A PROFESSIONAL GUIDE
TO MARKETING MANUSCRIPTS

BY PAUL R. REYNOLDS

The Writing and Selling of Non-Fiction
The Writing and Selling of Fiction
A Professional Guide to Marketing Manuscripts

A Professional Guide to Marketing Manuscripts

PAUL R. REYNOLDS

BOSTON / The Writer, Inc. / PUBLISHERS

A portion of this book originally appeared under the title, *The Writer and His Markets*. Several chapters were first published in *Saturday Review*.

Library of Congress Catalog Card Number   68-14751
Printed in the United States of America

CONTENTS

A PROFESSIONAL GUIDE
TO MARKETING MANUSCRIPTS

CHAPTER 1 ‖ BOOK PUBLISHING IN HARD COVERS

*E*VERY writer has to make his own decision as to what field he shall attempt to enter. Shall it be fiction or non-fiction or the drama? Does he want to be a book writer or a magazine writer or a dramatist for Broadway or for television or for motion pictures? Often the beginner experiments with one type of writing and then with another. Quite likely he tries short pieces before he tries a book—or he may never write a book.

However, the book is the basis of most writers' careers. Famous writers, name writers, writers who have influenced a broad public or have built up a wide reputation as entertainers have done this by being authors of successful books. (The only exception is a handful of Broadway dramatists who have made a reputation from their plays alone.) There are magazine writers in the fiction and non-fiction fields who make a good living year in and year out. There are skilled writers for motion pictures and for television, some of whom make an even better living. But such fiction, articles or screen plays do not bring to their creators any broad public recognition. A few dramatists excepted, it is almost impossible to mention any well-known writer whose reputation has not been made by his books. Book publication in the traditional form, printing between hard covers, is the foundation for a career in the world of the written word.

We therefore turn first to the trade book publisher, who

publishes fiction, non-fiction and juvenile books in hard covers.

If a trade book publisher accepts an author's manuscript for publication, he has read it (or has had it read by editors whose judgment he trusts), and has decided the public will pay to read it. He will therefore invest his own money into turning the manuscript into a book.

The publisher's first step after accepting a manuscript is signing a contract with the author. Then he must have the manuscript edited, the type set and proofread, a jacket designed and printed, and at least a minimum number of copies of the book printed and bound.

On the selling side, his problems are more diverse. He usually has a staff of salesmen (from seven to thirty or more) traveling from bookstore to bookstore, selling the books on his list. The publisher may have prepared posters or other display material for the bookstores. At the same time, he has placed a description of the book in his catalogue, and notices of the book, its price, date of publication, etc., in trade journals such as *Publishers' Weekly* and *American News of Books*. He may place one or more advertisements in such media. (For $420, he may purchase a page advertisement in *Publishers' Weekly*.) A month or so before publication, advance copies of the book are sent gratis to book reviewers all over the country; a few radio and television commentators may also be included on this review list. The publisher cannot hope to influence the opinion of the reviewers but he will attempt to get the book noticed and reviewed as prominently as possible. At the same time, he may issue a news release about the book or he may mail a circular praising the book to people who might be interested. On publication day the publisher may begin a small advertising campaign —perhaps three or four small advertisements in the New York *Times* Book Review section—or he may start advertising extensively. (A full page in the *Times* Book Review section costs $2,460.)

What does it cost a publisher to produce a book? In the case of a novel priced at $4.50, a publisher may give an average discount of 43 per cent. In other words, he collects from bookstores and others 57 per cent of the retail price of each copy sold. 57 per cent of $4.50 is $2.56½. If he prints five thousand copies and sells forty-five hundred, his costs and receipts might run somewhat as follows:

COSTS FOR PRINTING 5,000 COPIES

Plant (composition and plates)	$ 1,500
Manufacturing (paper, presswork, binding and jacket)	3,250
Advertising	1,000
Author's royalty (10 per cent of the retail price of the book—45¢—times 4,500, the number of copies sold)	2,025
Direct overhead (shipping charges, etc.)	630
	$ 8,405

RECEIPTS FROM SALE OF 4,500 COPIES

4,500 times $2.56½ is	$11,542.50

Subtracting the costs of $8,405 from the receipts of $11,542.50, we get the sum of $3,137.50 to go towards general overhead or profit.

The above figures are optimistic. Few novels with a printing of five thousand copies sell forty-five hundred copies. Average discounts for many publishers are higher than 43 per cent. The amount allotted above to advertising is minimal. However, these figures give a bird's-eye view.

Assuming that forty-five hundred copies are sold and paid for according to the foregoing figures, the publisher is better off in cash by $3,115. He is $3,115 richer than he would have been had he not published this particular book. But what about his general overhead? In the above figures the direct overhead, the increased overhead that this book caused, has been charged as a cost. No contribution to general overhead has been charged. Let us suppose the publisher publishes fifty books a year. Let us suppose his office rent, salaries of executives, editors, secretaries, proofreaders, stock clerks, salaries and traveling expenses of salesmen, interest on the capital invested in his business plus all the myriad other office expenses equal a total of $350,000 a year, a modest figure in these times. In order to pay this expense his fifty books must average a profit of $7,000 ($350,000 divided by 50 equals $7,000). If his fifty books show an average profit of only $3,115, he has $155,750 (50 times $3,115) towards his total overhead expense of $350,000. He has a loss for the fifty books published of $194,250 ($350,000 minus $155,750 equals $194,250).

A publisher may lose money as illustrated above. He may also lose in many specific instances. When a publisher advances money to an author, he debits the author's account and pays him no royalty until a sufficient number of copies have been sold to earn the advance. Many a book when published does not sell enough copies to earn half its advance. That part of the advance that is unearned must be absorbed by the publisher as an expense. $100,000 was advanced to Stanley High for his life of Billy Graham. The book did not earn $50,000 in royalties. This kind of gambling, whether in terms of a few thousand dollars or many thousands, occurs often. Many a gamble pays off; however, in a substantial number of cases there is a loss.

There are other losses. One of the curious things about the publishing business is that an experienced professional writer can often go to a publisher with an idea, sign a contract, and receive many thousands of dollars before he has written a word. Supposing a publisher advances an author $7,500 on a book to be written, and when the manuscript is delivered, it is not good enough to publish. The publisher has made a bad guess as to the potential ability of the author and he can only charge off the $7,500 to expenses. Sickness, or inability to get the material for a book, or death, may mean that a book on which money has been advanced never gets written. Sometimes downright dishonesty is involved. There are authors, fortunately few in number, who have received many thousands of dollars from one or more publishers and never delivered the books. In such a situation, a publisher occasionally will bring suit. But suing is an expensive business and often a judgment against an author cannot be collected. There is scarcely another business where a man, just by signing a piece of paper, can obtain substantial cash before doing any work. Publishers should probably have their heads examined for so conducting their affairs, but the competition for authors and manuscripts is keen and the practice is common.

A publisher loses money from copies of a book printed but unsold. Almost every book is delivered to the bookstores on consignment; that is to say, the bookstores may return to the publisher every copy which the public does not buy. If the publisher underprints and the bookstores are understocked, he can minimize his loss from copies returned unsold, but sales are lost because many of the bookstores run out of copies. If the publisher overprints, he gets a large number of copies back from the bookstores. The publisher can unload his unsold stock for a pittance (10¢ to—in rare cases—50¢ a copy) to a cut-rate dealer (this is called remaindering), but still his loss is great.

Sometimes a publisher has enormous returns. In 1964 William Morrow & Co. published a novel, *The Ordeal of Major Grigsby* by John Sherloch. The publishers printed some sixteen thousand copies and crammed them into the bookstores. Only about five thousand copies were sold to the public. Assuming the presswork, paper, and binding came to 75¢ a copy, Morrow had to absorb a loss of over $8,000 from such overprinting.

Although the average publisher loses money on many of

his books, he makes an enormous profit on a best seller. Morrow sold 167,741 copies of *The Shoes of The Fisherman* by Morris West. The publishers probably made 75¢ a copy or over $125,000 from the trade sale alone. Simon & Schuster's total profits on *The Rise and Fall of the Third Reich* by William Shirer were in excess of three quarters of a million dollars. Aside from the best seller (and the two above books were the biggest best sellers of their season), there is a good profit on a book which sells ten thousand copies or more. There are hundreds of such books published each year. They are the backbone of the industry.

Another source of profit to many a publisher is the continuing sale of the back list (books published in previous years). Orders for these older books flow in and are filled. No advertising is necessary and there is a profit on each copy sold. The old-line houses such as Houghton Mifflin, Alfred A. Knopf, and Little, Brown have many standard books still in copyright which bring them a large revenue. The cookbook *The Joy of Cooking,* the novels of Willa Cather, revised editions of Bartlett's *Familiar Quotations* are examples of books on back lists that continue to sell.

Despite the enormous profits from best sellers, despite the many profitable books in the 6,000 to 40,000 sales bracket, despite profitable back lists, few trade publishers in the last few years have shown profits on the sale of their books to bookstores and to libraries (juveniles excepted). The trade sale of the successful adult books does not make up for the lack of sale of the unsuccessful. Why isn't the publishing of adult trade books in the red? What makes this publishing profitable is one enormous source of income, a source not previously mentioned. The trade book publisher sells to paperback publishers and to book clubs the right to publish many of his books. The paperback publisher publishes the identical book in paperback for mass distribution via newsstands and stores. The book club publishes the identical book for sale by mail.

The trade book publisher retains in most cases 50 per cent of all such revenue, paying 50 per cent to the author. In 1966, the trade book publishers received in the aggregate from the paperback publishers a sum in excess of thirteen million dollars. The receipts from book clubs in the same year were in excess of four million dollars. An industry which otherwise would be almost bankrupt has become extremely profitable.

In the case of an individual title, the income from a paperback sale may be as large as the $500,000 paid for *Wanderers East, Wanderers West* by Kathleen Winsor, or as small as $1,000 paid for an obscure Western. And as of 1966, the Book-of-the-Month Club paid a minimum of $75,000 each month for its selection.

The fact that almost no trade book publisher year in and year out can show a profit without this extra paperback and book club revenue is, from an accountant's point of view, cockeyed. A publisher's capital—a million to several million dollars, depending upon size—is used to finance the acquisition of desirable manuscripts, their manufacture into bound volumes, and their sales through bookstores and to libraries. The publisher's employees expend their time and effort in these directions. Yet the profit for the operation depends upon something for which the publisher does not use his capital, and upon something which requires work from one or, at the most, two of his employees. The publisher may bargain with the paperbacks; bargaining is rare in the case of the book clubs. Most of the book clubs have standard and unvarying terms. All the publisher has to do is to offer the manuscript and wait for the book club lightning to strike. For this labor the publisher collects one-half of what may be enormous sums. From the point of view of the author, it is indefensible that as much as 50 per cent of the paperback and book club revenue from a novel should always remain with the publisher regardless of how well-known the author is or how profitable a bookstore sale the novel has.

A movement to change this started in 1964 and accelerated in 1965. The publisher's 50 per cent interest is now being reduced when the sums are enormous, and in some cases it is being eliminated. The big-name writers have had the bargaining power to insist on this. The new writer is also getting a better deal if he happens to strike the jackpot. W. W. Norton, the first publisher with the courage to publicly announce a new policy, has changed the publisher-author split in paperback income so that his authors will receive the following:

> 50 per cent of the first $10,000 paperback income, 55 per cent of the next $15,000, 60 per cent of the next $75,000, 65 per cent of the next $150,000 and 70 per cent thereafter.

In the case of a first novel or in the case of an author whose previous book sales have been modest, the fifty-fifty split of the first $5,000 or $10,000 collected is likely to remain for many years. A publisher is unlikely to publish such a book if he cannot foresee some extra paperback or book club income. However, as the pressure from authors grows and the fifty-fifty split is changed or eliminated, the trade book publisher will have to readjust his operation. Perhaps fewer unsuccessful books will be published. Perhaps ways will be found to reduce the publisher's overhead. Some of the old-line publishers privately admit that it may be better for the industry to learn to make a profit from its own functions of manufacturing, promoting, and selling hardback books. No publisher likes to see the disappearance of these thousands and thousands of dollars of unearned income, but the changing circumstances may well prove to be ultimately advantageous.

The juvenile department of a publisher is in a different category from his other trade books. Here there is little or no income from paperback and book club rights. Income arises from bookstore and library sales alone—primarily library sales (85 per cent of the sale of the average juvenile is made to libraries).

The publisher's profits from juvenile departments have been enormous in contrast to meager profits from adult books. There are several reasons for this. In the first place, the juvenile editor rarely commits himself or pays an author money before a satisfactory manuscript has been completed. Thus he avoids the dollar outlay and loss on contracts for books which never get written or on contracts for books which when written are not worthy of publication. Second, juvenile advances are moderate so that the unearned advances so costly to the publisher are rare in the juvenile field. There is also a saving because royalties on juveniles tend to be lower than the standard royalties for adult books. Furthermore, the juvenile publisher is seldom subject to the evil of overprinting and costly returns. (Libraries do not return books.) By working closely with the libraries and accepting only those manuscripts which conform to library standards, the publisher can predict the minimum sale with considerable accuracy. A further source of profit to the juvenile publisher is the back list. Juveniles may sell for years, chiefly to new libraries, or new branch libraries, or as replacements. This is in contrast to the average novel whose sale has stopped a year after publication.

The publisher of a juvenile can avoid an overexpenditure on advertising. In the case of the adult book mentioned before, *The Ordeal of Major Grigsby,* the publisher hoped for, expected, and wanted to stimulate a sale of twenty thousand or more copies; at the time of publication he spent more than $10,000 in advertising. As he sold only some five thousand copies, he spent over $2.00 in advertising for each copy sold, with a resulting large loss. No such misjudgment of sales and hence gross over-advertising is likely to occur with a juvenile.

One other factor adds to the profits of a publisher's juvenile department. The editorial overhead is lower. Juvenile editors and their assistants are usually women who command lower salaries than men. There are no expense account trips to

Europe as most juveniles are of American origin. Entertaining authors is relatively rare and less lavish than in other fields of publishing.

There were 2,375 new juveniles published in 1966. Some one hundred and fifty of these were written by professional writers of books for adults who wanted a change of pace and so did a book for children. The extremely successful Landmark series of biographies for young people published by Random House is written almost entirely by name writers in the adult field. Of the writers who specialize in juveniles, there are seventy-five to a hundred who make a reasonably good living. By regular production, book after book, these authors build up a following. A child who reads one book by such an author often goes back to the library and reads the other books so that each title helps the popularity of the other titles.

However, most writers of juveniles do children's books almost as hobbies for pin money. The majority of these writers do not remain permanently in the field. Perhaps they graduate to the adult field. Perhaps they have a good idea for their first juvenile but cannot repeat, and their further manuscripts remain unsold. Or perhaps they publish several juveniles but, finding that they are receiving little prestige and little money, they give up writing entirely. Sometimes this writing pays off, however. An outstanding Civil War novel, *Rifles for Watie*, was written by the publicity director of the University of Oklahoma football team, Harold Keith. Keith's previous juveniles had made little impact, but this book won the Newbery Medal (awarded annually for the most distinguished contribution to literature for American children), has sold in excess of eighty thousand copies, and will continue to sell for a long time.

Most publishers of hardback books also publish quality paperbacks. There is a big market for these in college bookstores. These quality paperbacks must be clearly distinguished from the mass-distributed paperbacks sold on newsstands. The newsstand item starts out with a printing rarely less than one hundred and fifty thousand copies and is usually an item of entertainment or of popular information. The most successful mass-distributed paperbacks are reprints of hardback best sellers. The quality paperbacks are generally higher priced than the mass-distributed paperbacks, and tend to be books of merit—scientific or literary titles with a present-day application. Sales of individual titles tend to run from ten to twenty thousand copies, royalties from 6 per cent to occasionally 8 per cent. With the low royalty and the low retail price, there is not much income in these for authors. As of now they are not an especially profitable line for the publisher, but the field is expanding. These books may be the precursors of a radical and permanent change in American publishing. Certainly, from the point of view of taste and culture, of scholarship and of learning, they are one of the most hopeful trends in the world of the written word.

The bane of the publishing industry are the thousand or more commercially unsuccessful books published each year, books whose sales in each case are under five thousand copies. The loss on such titles is severe. There are several reasons why failures get published. Often it is a matter of poor judgment; the publisher thought the book would attract readers and was proved wrong. Sometimes a poor book is published because the author's previous book was successful and the publisher does not want to lose the author to another publisher for the future. A bad first novel may be published because the publisher has faith in the author and believes that ultimately this author will write a successful book. Sometimes a poor book is published because the author is a friend of the publisher, or is in a position to bring the publisher good manuscripts by others, or is a friend of a best-selling author whom the publisher publishes. A book of quality may be published because the publisher believes it should be available even though its readership will be small and commercially it will not be successful. Sometimes a book is published because of financing on the part of an institution or business so that the publisher's basic costs are taken care of. At times a bad book is published because the publisher thinks he can make or already has made a good paperback sale so that the 50 per cent of the paperback revenue will cover the publisher's costs. This is most likely to occur when the chief appeal of the manuscript is sex. To what extent these inferior books follow Gresham's law—driving out the good books as inferior currency drives out the good currency—there is no way of ascertaining. Certainly inferior books do not help the industry.

Best sellers, major book club selections, books that command large advances from paperback outfits, or books that may sell in substantial quantities over a long period of years are hard to select and hard to obtain, and they make up less than 10 per cent of the books published. There have been no large fortunes made in the hardback book publishing industry, certainly none to compare with those made in magazine publishing, television, motion pictures, or even paperbacks. Salaries in the book publishing world are not high even though the qualities required for success—imagination, judgment, initiative and that sixth sense of feel for the whims of popular taste—are extremely rare. The great sellers of trade books, the successful heads of the great houses, probably would have made ten times as much money had they gone into the sausage or chewing gum business.

It is obvious that neither publisher nor author is sufficiently compensated in the case of the majority of published books. An author is apt to feel that the publisher would sell more copies of his book if the advertising were increased. In the sample publisher's budget given earlier in this chapter $1,000 was allotted for advertising. This would be the equivalent of two advertisements in the New York *Times* Book Review section of less than one-eighth of a page. Let us suppose that the publisher considers taking a further $500 advertisement in the *Times*. How many copies must this small advertisement sell in order for the publisher to recover his $500? If the publisher's cash intake over outgo for each copy sold is $1.50, he must sell as a result of the advertisement 334 copies to break even. Will one advertisement sell 334 copies? The publisher knows from long experience that it will not. One advertisement will not sell fifty copies because advertising does little directly to induce the public to buy books.

There was a concrete example of this in December, 1958. Fifteen days before Christmas all the New York City newspapers suspended publication because of a strike of delivery men. (Publication was resumed with the new year.) The New York City department stores suffered a severe decline in business, which they attributed to the absence of newspapers and newspaper advertising. Although there were no book review sections, no book advertising, and no book reviews published in New York during the peak of the Christmas season, New York City bookstores sold books as merrily as ever. There was no evidence of any appreciable decline in their business.

If advertising does not directly sell a lot of copies of a book, why do publishers advertise? A publisher may run an advertisement or two because of a guilty conscience. He feels that he must try to do something for each book he publishes. He may run an advertisement or two to please the author. Every author is flattered to see his title and his name in an advertisement. The publisher may advertise in the hope that his advertisements will impress other authors and their agents and thus bring him desirable manuscripts in the future. Those reasons for advertising are minor.

A publisher advertises because advertising affects the trade, with the indirect result that books get publicized, talked about, made available to the consumer and sold. What books are reviewed prominently in newspapers and magazines? What books are commented upon over the radio or on television?

What books are read—or at least looked at—by bookstore clerks, what books are recommended by them? What books are put in the store window or on the front shelf where many customers see them? Furthermore, what books are purchased by libraries? (It must be remembered that libraries account for 50 per cent of the total sale of many books for adults and the library sale increases as the bookstore sale increases.) The answer to each of these questions is: those books that are advertised. A bookstore clerk and a librarian know through experience that the heavily advertised books are usually the popular books, and hence are treated as potential best sellers. Books treated as potential best sellers usually sell well. As a general rule, best sellers are advertised heavily, moderate sellers are advertised moderately, and duds are advertised little if at all. It is hard to know whether the sales of a book cause the advertising or the advertising causes the sales, whether the chicken or the egg comes first.

A publisher has little problem selling books by "name" authors. Likewise, there is little problem in selling books by authors whose previous books have sold ten to twenty thousand copies. Many a reader who enjoyed an author's previous book will remember the author's name and read his next book. However, with a book by an unknown author the publisher has to start from scratch. None of the publisher's other books help him. Maybe the publisher has a best seller in a spy adventure story by Mr. X. This means nothing when one tries to determine whether the publisher can sell Mr. Y's spy adventure story.

Although a publisher has to start from scratch with each new book by an unknown author, he has one advantage over most other merchandisers. He can get his product reviewed, and unless it is extremely bad, praised free of charge in the news sections of the newspapers and magazines. A publisher gets thousands and thousands of dollars worth not only of free advertising but free advertising cooked up as news. This does not mean that there isn't competition for free review space; there is severe competition. The daily New York Times in 1966 reviewed some six hundred books out of several thousand offered for review. The Sunday Times Book Review section covers about twenty-five hundred titles a year. The individual book reviewer selects the books he will review on the basis of his guess as to their importance (future sale) and their general interest. He is influenced by the name of the author (some indication of the importance of the book), by a book club choice, by the imprint of the publisher (more negative than positive), by personal acquaintance and chitchat in the trade, and by an impressive advertising appropriation. Few if any newspapers or magazines refuse to review a book not advertised in their pages, none are so venal that they can be paid in advertising for a favorable review. But a heavy advertising appropriation is evidence that the book in question is important and probably will sell. Also, the individual reviewer knows that his colleagues on other papers will review any book heavily advertised, and hence such a book becomes news and must not be missed. Advertising gets books reviewed—not necessarily favorably reviewed, although most reviews (especially outside of New York City) tend to be favorable—but at least reviewed. Advertising helps get prominent reviews.

Do favorable reviews sell books? Not necessarily. In 1965, St. Martin's Press published *The Cultural Explosion* by Alvin Toffler. This book was reviewed favorably on the front page of the New York *Times* Book Review section and of the *Tribune* Book Review section, and was widely and favorably reviewed throughout the country. The total sale of this book was 3,734 copies. Every publisher has had similar experiences only too often.

Does publicity sell books? In March, 1960, a really fine book, *This is Where I Came In* by Edward Anthony, was published. Due to close friendship on the part of the author with the heads of both the Associated Press and the United Press, and due to certain timely news items in the book itself, feature articles praising the book ran in nearly every daily paper in America, many of them starting on the front page. The sale of the book was 1,718 copies.

If advertising and publicity do not in themselves directly sell books although they obviously often have an indirect effect, what does sell books? The answer is word-of-mouth comment. It is Mrs. Smith saying to Mrs. Jones, "Have you read so-and-so?" This sort of talk starts a book selling. Of course, word-of-mouth comment is a matter of degree. Occasionally it produces a best seller. In most cases it produces only modest sales. With no word-of-mouth recommendation, a book is almost certain to be a failure. How does a publisher get a large number of Mrs. Smiths to recommend a book? In the first place he must have the right book, the popular book, the book with the right words. Assuming the publisher has a good book, his problem is to get enough copies read at the start so that word-of-mouth recommendation has a chance to commence. Then the publisher tries to stimulate such word-of-mouth talk by getting the trade excited through advertising and publicity.

There is little that an author can do to aid the publisher in the sale of his book. The author can offer to write the blurb for the dust jacket. Most authors are too close to their work to be able to describe it objectively. A publisher with long experience in writing blurbs probably will do a better job. The author can see the advance sketch of the jacket painting; if he complains, a new sketch will probably be made which, when completed, is unlikely to sell more copies than the old idea would have. The author can agitate for more advertising, probably without success. He can trot around to bookstores and complain to the publisher that such and such a bookstore has no copies of his book. (The bookstore may have refused to buy copies but of course no bookstore will ever tell the author that.) The author can—if he has the money—hire a publicity firm to publicize himself and his book. He will be flattered by the publicity but this will probably sell few if any books that would not be sold anyway. Some authors make nuisances of themselves in one or more of the above ways, and possibly they get the publisher to do something not otherwise done. But an author who acts this way may kill his publisher's enthusiasm so that the publisher does less than he might otherwise have done.

On the other hand, the author who ignores his publisher and the publishing process loses something. Cultivating one's publisher in a nice sort of way without being a nuisance does pay off. Questions should be asked of the publisher and of his staff. Publishers can forget, can make mistakes, and should be kept on their toes. If in New York, why doesn't an author buy his editor a lunch? The editor will be pleased. In fact he will fall off his chair with surprise. Nineteen out of twenty authors expect their editors to pay for all lunches. Why doesn't an author take the person in charge of publicity out for a drink? Perhaps there are ways for the author to help publicize his own book. Why doesn't the author go to see the salesman who will be selling the book in his home city?

Should an author remain indefinitely with one publisher? Authors differ, publishers differ, and the relationships differ. The successful non-fiction writer often has to shift publishers because different publishers come to him with ideas for books and with offers he wants to accept. However, there are non-fiction writers who manage to stick to one publisher. For the novelist there is much to be said for finding a compatible publisher, who seems competent, and staying with him. If an author and a publisher can have a close relationship and friendship, the author has much to gain. Publishing is more than just manufacturing and distributing books. How much a publisher does in personally pushing a book (whether by word-of-mouth or through letters, or through formal promotion) is influenced by the personal relationship. For many authors there is another advantage to sticking to one publisher, an editorial one. Authors differ, but some like to discuss their work in advance of the writing. Some need encouragement, some the restraining hand. Some can benefit by the suggestions of a good editor for further revision of a completed manuscript. Editorial help is most beneficial when there is a close relationship between author and editor, and a genuine expectation on both sides of a continuing publishing relationship.

A close relationship between author and publisher requires a relaxed attitude and the attempt on the part of both to be fair in negotiating a contract. If the publisher is trying to obtain each book as cheaply as possible, or if the author is striving for the maximum contractual remuneration, friendship is damaged and effective cooperation becomes difficult. After all, hard bargaining between the president of a labor union and an industrialist is not conducive to friendship and future mutual help. The author and the publisher must look for an arrangement that seems fair to both parties. The publisher must be generous. The author must be fully aware that if he hunts he can always find some other publisher who will pay him a little more just to steal him. But the author also knows that the basis of his success is not the size of the advance or the rate of the royalty, but rather the largest possible sale in hard covers. This in the long run determines his prestige and the value of paperback rights, motion picture rights, serial rights, and foreign rights. Hence the enthusiasm of the publisher, and what the publisher does for the author's book above and beyond the call of duty, is of great value. Also, personal relations count for something to the author as a human being.

When should an author leave his publisher? Loyalty can be carried too far. In the 1930's, Bess Streeter Aldrich's books had an enormous vogue. She had picked a publisher named Appleton because the publisher's name, since it begins with

"A," was first on a list. The contracts for her books carried a fantastically low royalty and other poorish terms. An agent conveyed to her an offer from one of the best publishers in the country, an offer which probably would have doubled her income from her next book. She declined the offer, saying that she had used the same dentist, the same doctor, and the same lawyer all her life, and thought she would continue to use the same publisher. This attitude verges on the ridiculous.

The fifty-fifty split of paperback and book club rights is causing many best-selling authors to leave their publishers. If a publishing house has a rigid policy that it must retain one-half of all such revenue, and the amount is large, most authors, much as they may want to stay, would feel the pull of money, would feel that it was only intelligent to go to some other publisher not so greedy.

Another reason for leaving a publisher is if the author's editor leaves—and many editors in the last few years have been playing musical chairs, moving from one publishing house to another. Sometimes an author will follow his editor to the editor's new firm; sometimes the author may take the opportunity to explore the publishing field.

The best reason of all for an author to leave is if the author feels that his publisher is not doing a good job. The publisher may be treating the author too casually. Perhaps a new broom would be desirable. The author should ask himself what care the publisher is taking over the jacket and jacket copy. What is the publisher doing in the way of promotion outside of the routine? If the author is writing Westerns or mysteries, little special promotion can be expected, but still, what is the publisher doing? How imaginative does he seem? How efficient? How concerned over the author's books and the author's problems? It is not easy to answer these questions. But the answer (and the author should not expect the sky, or perfection) should determine whether to leave or stay. An author shouldn't be too critical or too complaisant.

In 1966, 5,085 new adult books of general interest were published in hard covers. (Text books, law books, and various other specialized books are not included in this total.) If we assume that the average author writes a book a year, some five thousand authors make their living or part of it from books. What does the average book earn from every source? There is no way of answering this question accurately, but here is a guess which has been checked with various editors and publishers and is, hopefully, an educated guess.

In 1966, the revenue from the publication of a book—revenue from all sources including advances against royalties, royalties, motion picture sales, foreign sales, etc.—amounted to:

more than $100,000 for seventy-five authors
more than $50,000 for one hundred authors
more than $20,000 for two hundred authors
more than $4,000 for fifteen hundred authors
less than $4,000 for thirty-five hundred authors.

Based upon the above, seven out of ten of the authors of books published in 1966 made little money for their effort, and yet not as little as appears. If we assume an author spends four hundred hours writing a book, and if his total remuneration is $2,000, his pay of $5.00 an hour (the pay of a carpenter or electrician) would not be sneezed at in many walks of life. Moreover, the book was probably written in the author's spare time while holding down another job, so that the $2,000 was extra income. There is also another benefit. A good carpenter or electrician may have the feeling of a job well done, but he would not speak of prestige in connection with his work. The author of nearly any published book, regardless of how small the sale, receives a certain amount of praise and prestige. I have met many authors dissatisfied with their publishers and with the sales of their books, but I can never recall meeting an author of a published book who regretted having undertaken the weary labor of composition even though his sale to the public was microscopic.

This chapter has dealt with authors in relation to commercial publishers, but it would not be complete without mentioning one sideline. A man who calls himself a "publisher", who is called in the trade a "vanity publisher", who wants to be called a "cooperative publisher", appears on the scene. These print-for-pay houses charge the author from $500 for a small pamphlet-length work to several thousand dollars for a full-length work, in exchange for which they arrange to put the manuscript into book form. These self-styled publishers praise what has been written although the manuscript may not be literate. They imply promotion and sales; they proffer an awe-inspiring contract. They agree to pay the author a large royalty, usually 40 per cent to 45 per cent on the contractual supposition that copies will be sold to the public and will earn a royalty. The entire arrangement is a gross travesty. These arrange-to-print publishers have no organization to sell books, and rarely if ever have any books that anyone will buy or read. The average sale of a book under contract with a "vanity" publisher is under one hundred copies, most of which are bought by the author, by his relatives, or by his friends. If a novel printed under the auspices of a vanity publisher has ever been sold to the movies, to a major book club, or even to a paperback, there is no record of such a sale. Certainly, the book would be under a cloud with such markets. A sale would be more likely from a manuscript copy rather than from a subsidized printed copy.

Book publishing is an old, established business. There are old-line houses of standing today who have been operating for two or more generations. The publisher's methods of doing business have not changed substantially in sixty years. Little research is done as to markets or selling practices or more efficient methods of distribution of books. If publishers are old-fashioned and shackled by tradition, their business ethics are high. Royalty statements of all the established trade publishers are accepted without question as truthful and honest. Considering the speculative nature of the business, and its attraction for amateurs, bankruptcy has been a rare occurrence. Contracts entered into are honored; a publisher's word is in general considered good.

Nevertheless, current publisher-author relations leave much to be desired. There are a number of publishers who will draw a stiff contract with an unknown author willing to sign almost anything for the sake of publication. These same houses will sign a fair contract in the case of an unknown author who knows the customs of the trade or who is handled by one of the leading literary agents. Moreover, many publishers will pay one royalty rate to one author and a higher rate to another author who drives a hard bargain, even though the sales records of both authors are approximately the same.

Book publishers have made few attempts to promote good relations with authors. Although there are exceptions, by and large publishers are secretive and evasive about their business methods. The average publisher would be horrified if the author suggested that the publisher give a profit-or-loss balance sheet as far as the author's own book was concerned. *The New Yorker* magazine has for years operated a trust or pension plan for its writers. It does not seem to have occurred to any publisher to develop a similar plan. No publisher seems to have considered profit-sharing with authors until in January, 1966, George Brockway of W. W. Norton & Co. announced a 5 per cent bonus to his authors as a result of the firm's large profits in the previous year. Publishers have been taking 50 per cent of enormous paperback and book club revenue, and as far as the author of this volume knows, not a single publisher has ever raised his voice on the ground that such conduct was unfair to the author.

However there is another side to the coin. Publishers have a pride in their occupation. Alfred A. Knopf has spent thou-

sands and thousands of dollars on the makeup and appearance of his books, for which he cannot conceivably expect
a financial return. More than one publisher has published a
book which will not make money but which the publisher
believes should be published as a public service. Occasionally
an author is helped financially because the publisher believes in him, even though the publisher sees little prospect
of a return. There is no other writer's medium where there is
even an iota of this kind of idealism.

CHAPTER 2 ‖ THE BOOK CONTRACT

O_{NCE} a book is accepted for publication, the author is presented with a long and complicated contract for his approval and signature. These contracts are monstrosities of legal verbosity. The Alfred A. Knopf contract contains about twenty-eight hundred words, the Harper contract, about three thousand, the Simon & Schuster contract—the longest of all—nearly five thousand words.

Many things which are implied in the author-publisher relationship are left unmentioned in the usual contract, however. There is no requirement in the average contract that the publisher must publish the author's work as the author wrote it without any changes being made by the publisher. There have been cases where publishers without permission from authors have rewritten parts of books, but such cases have been very very rare. Any such activity is contrary to custom and to the ethics of the industry. On the other hand, it is usual and expected that the publisher should copy-edit the manuscript; that is, correct spelling, punctuation, capitalization, bad grammar, etc. Recently a publisher misspelled an author's name, not on the jacket, not on the title page, but on the spine of the book. The author was furious and wrote indignantly to her agent because there was nothing in the contract requiring the publisher to spell her name correctly. In this case the publisher expressed his sorrow over the mistake but pointed out that it could not be of too great consequence as neither the author nor any member of his family had removed the jacket and noticed the error until three months after publication.

The nucleus of the contract between author and publisher —and what the author must study—is the following:

1. The advance or cash money the author is to receive and when he is to receive it.
2. The rate of royalty (that is, the number of cents per each copy sold that the author is to receive).
3. The rights given to the publisher other than North American Book rights and the per cent of interest the publisher has in such rights.
4. Under what conditions, if any, the publisher can get out of his apparent obligations to pay further money.
5. To what extent the author is committed to the publisher for any future books the author may write.

Assuming the contract is one offered by the forty or so well-known publishers, the author need not concern himself with anything else but these five items. The mass of other stipulations in the contract are probably unfair to the author (they have been drawn up by the publisher's lawyer and are weighted in the publisher's favor). But in ninety-nine cases out of one hundred all these extra clauses are trivial and unimportant.

1. The advance

The advance against hoped-for royalties on the ordinary trade book is seldom less than $1,000—and usually considerably more. This is money the author gets and may keep regardless of how few copies of the book are sold. The advance may be paid upon signing of the contract, or upon publication, or split between the two dates. How much larger an advance than $1,000 the author can obtain depends upon the publisher, upon the publisher's estimate of the value of the manuscript, and—if the author has had previous books published—upon the publisher's estimate of the value of the author's reputation. The publisher's business generosity plus the author's or his agent's bargaining ability are also factors. Publishers differ greatly in their evaluations. In the case of an important book one publisher's offer to an author may differ from another publisher's offer by thousands and thousands of dollars.

From the author's point of view, the higher the advance the better. In the first place, money in hand is money in hand. Many a book does not sell as well as the publisher expects, and hence royalty and earnings will be small.

There is another reason for a large advance. It is an indication of what the publisher plans to do for the book. If a publisher expects a book to sell no more than five thousand copies, he will advance the author only a small sum. If a publisher plans to make a book his leader for fall publication, if he plans to advertise a book heavily, expecting large sales, he will usually be willing to advance the author a sizable sum. An author wants to find a publisher who will promote his book extensively. A large advance does not insure this but makes it probable. What is the maximum advance possible? Advances can be any sum up to (in extreme cases with an extraordinarily popular author) half a million dollars.

2. The rate of royalty

Book royalty on the average adult trade book is seldom lower than 10 per cent of the retail price and rarely higher than 15 per cent. Average royalties for a first novel with one of the top publishers would be 10 per cent on the first five thousand copies sold, $12\frac{1}{2}$ per cent on the next five thousand copies sold, and 15 per cent on all copies sold thereafter. A juvenile with expensive illustrations usually has a royalty of less than 10 per cent. A novelist whose previous books have sold over ten thousand copies can usually command a straight 15 per cent royalty. Some enormously popular authors have obtained royalties of $17\frac{1}{2}$ per cent or even 20 per cent.

Nearly every contract calls for accounts to be rendered and payment of royalties to be made every six months. Some publishers prefer to pay a royalty of from 15 per cent to 25 per cent of the wholesale price; *i.e.*, on what the publisher receives for the book rather than what the public pays. Theoretically this is a fairer way of computing the author's remuneration, but it has the disadvantage of making it difficult for the author to figure how much money he will receive from the sale of a specific number of copies. The author does not know what discounts the publisher is giving, and hence what the wholesale price is. Some publishers have used this method of computation as a way of concealing a reduced remuneration to the author.

In every contract there are standard provisions for a lower royalty in particular cases. For example, a royalty of 5 per cent is paid on mail order sales made not through a book club but by the publisher. This percentage is probably too low but only certain types of specialized non-fiction books such as non-fiction sex books or how-to-do-it books can be sold by mail. Likewise, sales in Canada or overseas are usually at one-half royalty. No royalty is paid on books given away for promotion purposes and sales made at below cost of manufacture, which is fair enough. In the case of most books, none of these exceptions is important, or is likely to make much difference to the author's revenue.

However, there is one exception in many publishers' form contracts which every author should watch for. This is the clause to the effect that on any book which the publisher sells at a discount of 50 per cent or more (normal discounts run from 43 per cent to occasionally 48 per cent) the author is to receive 10 per cent of the wholesale price, that is, 10 per cent of what the publisher collects. This is the equivalent of a 5 per cent royalty or less on the retail price of the books. Such a clause is pernicious, not merely because it reduces the author's remuneration by more than one-half, but also because it offers the publisher a financial inducement to sell books at a discount of 50 per cent or more. The publisher's saving in royalty greatly exceeds his loss from the higher discount. Howard Fast figured that he lost over $2,500 because the publisher sold some seven thousand copies of his book at a 55 per cent discount and under this pernicious clause paid him the equivalent of a $4\frac{1}{2}$ per cent royalty.

A publisher who sells copies at an unusually high discount is entitled to pay a lower royalty. The following clause copied from the William Morrow & Co. contract covers the situation in a fair fashion:

> Where the discount to wholesalers, retail distributors, book clubs, reading circles or special markets in the U.S.A. is 48 per cent, a rate of royalty 1 per cent lower than the prevailing rate and with each additional 1 per cent in discount, the rate shall be further reduced by an additional one-half of 1 per cent. In no case, however, shall the royalty be less than one-half of the prevailing rate.

3. The rights given to the publisher

When an author arranges for the publication of his book, he thinks of the publisher as selling the book in the United States and Canada, and paying a royalty on each copy sold. Selling books to libraries and to the public via bookstores is the publisher's job. However, the typical publisher's book contract gives the publisher other rights, rights which may be of enormous value. The most important of these rights are the paperback and book club rights, which have been previously discussed.

Most form contracts give the publisher the right to sell second serial rights (this is the right to sell the book to newspapers and magazines after book publication), and foreign rights (the right to arrange for publication in England and in translation all over the world). The publisher's interest in second serial rights is usually 50 per cent. Such rights are rarely of much value. In the case of foreign rights, the publisher's interest may be 50 per cent, or sometimes it is only 25 per cent. Often the publisher first deducts a commission for the foreign representative who sold these rights, so that the author's take may be considerably less than the allotted per cent. Foreign rights may be of large value. For example, a good mystery novel may make much more money in Europe in translation than it makes in royalty in the United States. However, it is difficult for the average author to sell translation rights himself. Unless or until he puts his work in the hands of an agent, the author had better let the publisher manage these foreign publications.

Many publishers also ask for the right to sell the first serial rights (publication in a magazine before book publication) and motion picture rights. Again, if the author has no agent, the publisher probably should control these rights, but regardless of what per cent of these rights the publisher suggests, his interest should not be greater than 10 per cent. Most publishers will so agree if the author shouts loud enough.

4. The publisher and his obligations

When an author sells a publisher a completed manuscript, the publisher pays money down and agrees to publish; the author can therefore feel reasonably certain of publication. The situation is different when an author signs a contract with a publisher on the basis of an idea or outline. In such a case the contract probably calls for something to be paid upon signing (perhaps half of the total advance) and the balance of the advance upon delivery of the completed manuscript. Suppose the publisher does not like the finished manuscript. In practically every book contract there is a sentence in fine print (nearly everything in a book contract is in fine print) which states that the publisher need not pay any further money unless the manuscript is satisfactory, *i.e.*, satisfactory to the publisher in his sole judgment. This is unfair. The publisher's opinion of the manuscript may be unsound. The editor who signed up the author may have lost his job during the year or more that the author was writing the book, and the new editor may be unsympathetic to the project and want out. Or the publisher may have changed his mind and decided not to invest money in this manuscript for business reasons. In any such case the author will not get publication or even the balance of his advance.

There is no practical way of forcing a publisher to publish a manuscript he doesn't like. If the author can get the word *satisfactory* deleted, he will be able to collect the money due, and then, if necessary, look for another publisher. If the publisher refuses to delete the word *satisfactory* (and most will refuse), the author should try to have as much money as possible paid to him before delivery of the manuscript.

5. Commitment of future books

Most book contracts give the publisher an option to publish the author's next work or works. This clause is advantageous to the publisher in that he may get a good next book, and yet he is not obligated to pay out money or to publish if he doesn't like the next book. This clause may bring a certain advantage to the author. A publisher may do more to promote a book and build up the reputation of the author if the publisher expects to have further books by that author. A publisher may think of himself as building up a property. However the option should be only for one book, the next book. Publishers change, their staffs change, and an author should not be committed too far ahead. Most publishers will usually settle for an option on one book. An option to publish the next book may be at the same terms as the previous book, or it may be at terms to be arranged at the time of delivery of the next book. An option to publish at the same terms as the first book is unfair to the author. The next book manuscript may warrant different and much better terms. Many an author has been seriously damaged financially by this option at-the-same-terms clause. Thornton Wilder wrote a novel entitled *The Cabala* which had a small sale. He then delivered to his publisher a new book, *The Bridge of San Luis Rey.* A month after publication, he wrote an agent saying that his friends told him *The Bridge of San Luis Rey* was selling to the public and shouldn't he have a contract? Investigation disclosed that Mr. Wilder had sold *The Cabala* at poor terms with a clause in the contract that his publisher had an option on the author's next two books at exactly the same poor terms. Hence Mr. Wilder did not need a new contract for *The Bridge of San Luis Rey.* The terms and everything else were settled in the contract for *The Cabala. The Bridge of San Luis Rey* had an enormous sale, and won the Pulitzer Prize. The author's name, Thornton Wilder, acquired great value. Had Mr. Wilder refused to accept the option clause in his contract for *The Cabala,* he could have made much more money from much better contracts for his two succeeding books.

Few publishers will insist upon the obnoxious at-the-same-terms clause, and no author should sign a contract with that clause in it.

CHAPTER 3 ‖ MASS-DISTRIBUTED PAPERBACKS

*W*E have discussed, in the previous chapters, traditional book publishing—that is to say, an author's creation, printed and bound in hard covers, sold by the publisher primarily to bookstores and to libraries. This medium is what develops name writers, brings prestige, and is the basis of most writing careers. We have also discussed a corollary to hardback publishing, the quality paperback whose problems, although different from the hardback, run along the same general lines. There is a markedly different form of publication, also called a book, namely the mass-distributed low-priced paperback publication. This low-priced paperback sold on newsstands, in drug stores, in bookstores, and in many other places, is the subject of this chapter.

Mass-distributed paperback publication is an industry in itself, and one of sizable proportions. The traditional publisher of a hardback book retailing at $4.00 or more occasionally will have a semi-mass circulation title, a book that sells one or two or even three hundred thousand copies—a national best seller. He loves it when he does have such a book, but he can and, on the whole, does exist on sales of from five thousand to twenty-five thousand copies per title. His business is geared to those relatively low sales. The mass-distributed paperback publisher must always have a mass market. His minimum printing of one title cannot be less than seventy-five thousand copies and usually is more. With a best-selling novel by a name author, the first printing may be a million copies and perhaps two million will eventually be sold.

The paperbacks represent a direct market for authors. In 1966, four hundred seventy-eight manuscripts were sold to paperback firms for first publication. Most of these books were mysteries, Westerns, science fiction, adventure, or bad novels loaded with sex. The author of an original paperback gets from $2,000 to (rarely) $5,000 as an advance against a royalty which is usually 4 per cent on the first one hundred and fifty thousand copies sold and 6 per cent thereafter. In four out of five cases the book does not sell enough copies to earn its advance or pay the author any further royalties. Theoretically, an original paperback might sell a million copies, and there have been a handful of such cases—mostly in the non-fiction field. Usually, even if the book earns its advance, there is only a dribble of additional money for the author.

Original publication in paperback is less exciting than hard-back publication. There are few reviews of a paperback, little advertising, and for the author little prestige. Neither the author's friends nor anyone else is likely to hear of the book.

If the author of original paperbacks is to make any kind of living, he must be able to write rapidly, deliver a good finished product without much time-consuming rewriting, and turn out four or five completed manuscripts a year. The length of each novel is usually from fifty to seventy thousand words. The product may be published under the author's name or under one or more pen names. The paperback publisher has the same relation to the author as a hardback publisher, but his is a more sloppy operation. Copy editing is at a minimum, and galleys are often not shown to the author for correction.

Why does an author sell his manuscript for first publication in paperback? Why doesn't he sell it to a hardback publisher? The author often goes to a paperback first because he cannot find a hardback publisher who will accept his manuscript. Also, with a certain type of book such as a routine Western, the author may be better off financially with just paperback publication. If the author of a second-rate book sells to a hardback publisher, the author must let that publisher have 50 per cent of the paperback revenue. Hardback advance and royalty plus 50 per cent of paperback reprint may be less than the author's income might be from a first publication paperback.

However, when an author has written a good novel or good non-fiction book, he should always try for hardback publication first with the hope or expectation that paperback publication will follow. It is in hardback that there is the possibility for the big prize in prestige and money. There may be a substantial hardback sale with large royalties accruing. There may be a book club selection (book clubs never accept paperbacks). There may be a large paperback sale following the hardback sale. Let us look at the record of a first novel which was by no means a best seller, *The Q Document* by John Hall Roberts. The author received:

$ 2,876 royalty from sale in hardback
$ 6,000 one-half of Dollar Book Club revenue
$16,500 one-half of the advance from paperback reprint
$25,376 total remuneration

If this novel had been sold as an original in paperback, the author might possibly have received as much as $5,000 as an advance and probably would never have seen a penny more in royalty. His prestige from the paperback publication would have been almost nil.

Publishing original manuscripts in paperback is a small part of the business. What the industry depends upon is the reprinting of thousands of hardback books in paperback at a cheap price. In 1966, three-fourths of all published paperback titles were reprints of books published a year or more earlier in hardback. But this is only part of the story. The reprint paperback on the newsstand far outsold the average original.

There are two reasons why paperback reprints sell so well. First, the paperback reprint is a known product. It has been publicized by being published in hardback. Secondly, it is more apt to be a good product. It has been tested in hardback.

There are five large paperback firms—Bantam, Dell, Fawcett, New American Library, and Pocket Books—each with widespread distribution. There are twice as many smaller firms. The competition among these firms to acquire good titles for reprint is severe. The hardback publishers spur on the competition. They offer galleys or bound copies of their books simultaneously to every big paperback buyer. In the case of each title the hardback publisher asks for bids, gives a deadline, and usually takes the highest offer. Of course he may jockey around, playing one firm against another. It is like an auction, with all the factors which make it possible for the auctioneer to obtain a large price.

When a paperback publisher buys the rights to a book from a hardback publisher, he usually is not permitted to publish in paperback until at least a year after the first publication in hardback. Release in paperback kills the hardback sale in bookstores. *The Shoes of The Fisherman* by Morris West was still on the best seller list a year after its publication in hardback and selling over one thousand copies a week. Upon Dell's release in paperback, the hardback sale abruptly ceased. If Dell's release had been postponed, many more thousands of copies of the hardback edition would have been sold.

The paperback publishers lack the extra sources of income available to the hardback publisher. Paperback publishers have no income from libraries, little or no income from the sale of books on a back list, and little income from the sale of other rights such as the unimportant second serial rights or the much more valuable book club rights. Their profits arise from their primary occupation of selling paperbacks to the public via newsstands.

The profits from publishing a paperback which sells only one hundred thousand copies are modest, perhaps $5,000. What keeps the profits down is the cost of manufacturing and distributing copies which never get sold. Paperbacks are sold to newsstands on a consignment basis. What the newsstands cannot sell to the public, they destroy and do not pay for. If a paperback prints and distributes one hundred fifty thousand copies, he is often lucky if one hundred thousand copies are sold. Obviously, in such a situation, the paperback publisher cannot afford to pay much for the rights to publish—and he doesn't.

Publishing a best seller in paperback, publishing a book whose sales run from half a million to possibly two million copies, brings fantastically different results. Here returns (percentage wise) are much less and the unit cost for manufacture and distribution goes down sharply. A 95¢ paperback book which sells a million copies might show a profit (expense of obtaining rights not included) of $350,000 (give or take $25,000 depending upon the costs of a particular book). If the paperback publisher pays $300,000 for the rights to a title per the above figures and sells a million copies, he is better off by $50,000 than he would have been had he not published this particular title. The competition for the good titles which may sell a million or more copies is severe. Hence the paperback publisher often has to pay the hardback publisher an astronomical sum for a good book. $700,000 was paid for *The Source* by James Michener. Payments of such amounts leave the publisher with little profit unless the sale is phenomenal, two million or more. If the market is misjudged and only a million copies are sold, the publisher may have a severe loss.

Three of the major paperback firms—Dell, New American Library, and Pocket Books—have gone into the publishing of hardback books as well as paperback. These three firms purchase from the author at the start both hardback and paperback rights. They hope in this way to obtain titles for paperback reprint less expensively. Each of these houses took a substantial loss on their hardback publishing venture in 1966. It is too early to determine whether they can get their hardback operation on a paying basis in the future, or whether their hardback line will bring them a sufficient number of good properties for paperback to justify publishing hardback books at a loss.

One would expect that the enormous distribution and readership of paperbacks would materially cut into the sale of hardback books. Certainly the readership of fiction in hardback has been slowly declining in the last few years, while the readership of fiction in paperback has been increasing fantastically. Non-fiction has shown an increased appeal in both hardback and paperback.

The paperback industry is a new industry with its traditions not yet crystallized. New methods of manufacture and sale are continually being sought, and new practices evolved. The men running the paperback firms have the drive the old-line hardback publishers often lack. On the other hand, the paperback firms lack what at least some of the hardback publishers have, a feeling that their industry has a public purpose.

Of course, there are notable exceptions but the motion picture and television media have become, by and large, a vulgarizing influence upon public taste—the enemies of art and culture and man's ennoblement. No such statement can be made with regard to the paperback publishers. More and more they are increasing by millions the readership of books previously published in hardback. It is true that the paperbacks have emphasized, in many cases, the debasing side of sex in its clinical details, and have done this perhaps somewhat more than the hardbacks. But when one observes a sale of over two million copies of *The Rise and Fall of the Third Reich* and a sale of over a million copies of *The Devil's Ad-*

vocate by Morris West—books of quality to all people of discernment—one can only praise the medium. What sells in paperback is what sells in hardback—good books, bad books, and indifferent books. There is no indication that the readership of good books is on the decline.

CHAPTER 4 || *THE BOOK CLUBS*

BOOKS are sold to libraries. They are sold to the public through bookstores, via newsstands (in paperback editions), and they are also sold by mail. One form of mail-order selling of books, namely via a so-called book club, has in the last twenty years grown into one of the great industries of the publishing world. In 1965 there were 105 adult book clubs which distributed more than 1,500 titles.

As far as the average author is concerned, the arrangement for a book club edition is similar to the arrangement for a paperback edition. The publisher, through his contract with the author, obtains the book club rights. The publisher then sells to the book club the right to use the title in question. An advance against royalties is collected from the club, the money being split fifty-fifty with the author. Advances range from a minimum of $1,000 to a maximum in several cases in excess of $100,000. The size of the advance is governed by the circulation of the club, and occasionally by the importance of the title chosen. In most cases, the publisher does no bargaining; the club's terms are standard and not subject to improvement. The publisher offers his manuscript or galley proofs and waits for the club lightning to strike.

There is little variation to a book club's operation. People are circularized by mail. Coupon advertising is run. Those who subscribe are sent the monthly or quarterly selection of the club. In some cases two or more books are included in one volume. Subscribers obligate themselves to buy a stipulated number of books a year, but if they do not want the title proffered usually they can pick some other title, or they can let a month or more pass without taking any book. Subscribers often receive a free book when they subscribe, and after they have paid for a certain number of books, further free books, called dividends, may be sent to them. Book clubs have an enormous turn-over. In the case of the three largest clubs, thousands and thousands of new subscribers must be found each year to replace the ones who withdraw. On the other hand, the collection problem is slight. Over 95 per cent of the subscribers pay.

Subscribing to a book club is the easy way of buying a hardback book. The subscriber is saved the trouble of going to a bookstore, which may be far from his home. His books are picked for him by alleged experts and arrive with the postman, accompanied by lavish circulars justifying and praising the selection. Moreover, the subscriber obtains the book at a price substantially lower than he would have to pay for the same volume in a bookstore. The last is a big factor in the success of the industry.

Book clubs are able to offer their selections at a relatively low price because of mass circulation. Unit cost per volume goes down as the printings increase. Moreover, a book club pays a low royalty for the rights. Most important of all, the club collects the full amount paid by the customer. There is no discount to a retailer. Selling by mail is expensive, but less expensive than the cumbersome methods of the original publisher, whose salesmen—metaphorically speaking—ring bookstore bells and offer their wares like the peddler of old.

The Reader's Digest Condensed Books is the club with the largest distribution, and, in relation to the capital invested, is the most profitable individual book club in the country. This book club was started in the spring of 1950. Four books were condensed to make a volume of one hundred ninety-two thousand words. Three million subscribers to the *Reader's Digest* magazine were solicited by mail as to whether they wanted to become subscribers to the book club. Some one hundred and eighty thousand responded favorably. Since then, every three months (or four times a year) a volume consisting of from four to seven condensations has been sent to the subscribers. As the club grew, solicitation was made on an even wider basis than the magazine subscription list, although today the subscription list remains the basis. By January, 1966, three million subscribers to the book club were enrolled. During the year 1966, the club paid publishers a total sum of $2,000,000 for the right to use the books selected and published in the four volumes. What was paid for an individual title depended upon the number of words used in the condensed form, and upon the Digest's judgment as to the value of the author's name. The Digest is always the sole arbiter as to how the pie is cut.

The amazing growth of the Reader's Digest Condensed Books has been due in part to the Digest name. The club has a competitive advantage over other clubs because it can circulate the sixteen million subscribers to the *Reader's Digest* magazine, a substantial number of whom start off with a feeling akin to affection for anything with the *Reader's Digest* name upon it, and hence tend to join the book club.

The Digest proffers a good-looking hardback book illustrated in color with more reading matter than is contained in the average hardback or paperback. However, the chief cause of the success of this club is the packaging of four to seven condensed books in one volume at a price of $2.10. To buy these books individually in hardback would cost the purchaser over thirty dollars, in paperback, over three dollars. True, the Digest condenses the books, but still, it is quite a bargain at $2.10. Actually, the cost is even further reduced by the offer to join the club. For ten cents a subscriber can obtain the first volume, providing he agrees to buy the next three volumes at $2.10 each. The Reader's Digest Condensed Books offer the reader more for less money than does any other club.

The Digest money is so great that authors have not objected to their work being cut, condensed, or even mutilated, so as to be suitable for the Digest Book Club edition. Only one author and publisher have refused to permit a book to be cut or altered. When the Digest offered to accept for their club *A Single Pebble* by John Hersey, the publisher, Alfred A. Knopf, possibly at the request and certainly with the permission of the author, refused to allow a word of the novel to be changed or eliminated. The book was short, approximately thirty-five thousand words. The Digest Club included this book in its volume exactly as it was written and printed in the bookstore edition. People who love the written word and believe an author's work should be published as written must pay a tribute to this author and to this publisher.

The Reader's Digest Book Club receives manuscripts, galleys, and bound volumes before or after publication from any and every source. The English publisher, William Collins, contracted for British Empire rights to a novel by an Australian, Jon Cleary, entitled *The Green Helmet*. Collins promptly submitted the manuscript to the *Reader's Digest*. The Digest accepted the book for its book club even though no American publisher had seen or contracted for the manuscript. Collins received one thousand pounds (about $2,800) for his activity in submitting the manuscript, which money Collins did not pay to the author (not even half was paid to the author). Collins just pocketed the money received for giving the Digest a good tip. There was no legal or contractual obligation requiring Collins to pay the money—or part of it—to the author as Collins did not possess and hence could not arrange for or sell American book club rights. In due course, the manuscript was accepted and published by William Morrow & Co. Of course, the Digest would have seen the manuscript later from Morrow, but the Digest was glad to give one thousand pounds to Collins who sent the manuscript to them first. There is so much money around that money means little to the Digest; financial encouragement to English publishers means a lot.

The most successful book-club empire, because of the number of its clubs and the total volume of its business, is the Doubleday Book Clubs. Books are selected for approximately two dozen clubs, and a book selected for one is usually sold a little in one or more of the other clubs. In 1966, the combined clubs sent out a total of approximately two thousand different titles. The clubs paid publishers in excess of $4,000,000, half of which in most cases was distributed among the authors. Of these authors, about thirty received $20,000 or more.

Of all the Doubleday clubs, the most important financially to publisher and author is the Literary Guild, which in 1966 had an average circulation of 175,000 copies per month. The Guild pays advances on its selections ranging from $35,000 to $100,000 or more. Average earnings of a Guild selection run to about $65,000. Occasionally a Guild selection may earn a fantastic sum, especially when it is used in Guild advertising over a period of years.

Of the three major book clubs, the Digest holds the record for the largest individual circulation, the Literary Guild is noted as the leader of the largest book-club empire, and the third, the Book-of-the-Month, has a distinction of its own: a distinction in its selections and a reputation superior to either of its rivals for the quality of the books it circulates. The Book-of-the-Month was founded in 1926, and until World War II was the undisputed leader in the field. In the last twenty years, despite the rise of its competitors, it has survived and grown, and done this without cheapening its product. In 1965, this club had an average membership of 600,000, and paid each publisher of its twelve selections a minimum advance of $75,000 against a royalty of 10 per cent of the price per copy.

This club operates differently from the others. Books are submitted to the club by publishers in galley form. Each month, the management selects five or six books as candidates for a selection. These candidates, called in the trade "A" books, are sent to the judges who pick one of them as the Book-of-the-Month. For readers who do not like the selection, an alternate is chosen, but such choice is made by the management. Just as the management has nothing to do with the club selection (other than choosing possible candidates), so the judges have nothing to say as to the alternate selection. Likewise, give-away or dividend books and recommended books are selected by the management.

Perhaps because of the judges, perhaps because of a policy continued from the beginning, the club's selections are more literary, more distinguished, and have greater appeal to the discerning reader than those of either the Reader's Digest Condensed Books or the Literary Guild. The authors of Book-of-the-Month selections during the last twenty years read like a galaxy of the most distinguished American and British authors. Pearl S. Buck, C. S. Forester, John Steinbeck, John Gunther, and John Hersey have had two or more selections. Winston Churchill has had nine selections.

Aside from the three major book clubs there were, as of 1966, 102 minor clubs. Each year new minor clubs are started and each year a certain number prove unprofitable and are disbanded. One minor club in the Doubleday chain, the Dollar Book Club, with an average circulation of 675,000, is of real importance financially to publisher and author. Many of the minor clubs are very specialized in their choices—for instance, the four Catholic clubs, the two mystery clubs, the History Book Club, the Outdoor Life Book Club, etc. Certain minor clubs have a distinction which brings to the author not merely added readers, not merely added money, but added prestige.

It is not unusual for a book to be chosen by more than one club. The Literary Guild and the Book-of-the-Month seem to be in direct competition and rarely take each other's choices, but neither strenuously objects to the Reader's Digest Condensed Books. A mystery story may be the latter's selection and also a selection of one of the mystery book clubs. Any book selected by one of the Doubleday clubs is to a certain extent sold through them all. Occasionally a formal Guild selection and a formal Dollar selection will be the same title. Sometimes a title will be selected by more than one minor club.

There is a direct relationship between major book club selection and best sellers. At least half the best sellers of 1966 were major book club selections. Book clubs try to select books which will be popular with their readers, and, to the extent they have selected well, they have selected books which will be popular in the bookstores. Moreover, when a book is chosen by a major book club, the publisher knows that this book is certain to show him a large profit (his share of the book club money is $20,000 to $50,000). Hence he can afford to advertise the book profusely and often does. This enhances the bookstore sale.

The book clubs differ as to their direct effect on the bookstore sale. Selection by the Reader's Digest Condensed Books seems to have no effect whatsoever on the bookstore sale. Their club's public is not a bookstore buying public. Selection by the Literary Guild seems to hurt the trade sale, but only a little. In most cases at least some Guild subscribers would have bought the book in a bookstore had they not received it as a Guild selection. Selection by the Book-of-the-Month inevitably helps the trade sale. Potential buyers may be lost because they are subscribers to the Book-of-the-Month Club, but for every buyer lost, two new buyers are created. These new buyers appear because of the prestige connected with the club (it becomes fashionable to read the book) and because of the extra hullabaloo generated by the club's choice. Some of the minor clubs such as the Junior Literary Guild and possibly the Dollar Book Club seem to have an adverse effect on the bookstore sale.

The author, although so vitally concerned, has almost no direct relation to the book clubs. Certain agents will show manuscripts to the Reader's Digest Condensed Books and occasionally to the minor book clubs. The Doubleday Book Club empire operates almost exclusively through publishers, and the Book-of-the-Month, making their decisions by reading galleys, cannot seriously consider a manuscript from an author or an agent. Nevertheless, the leading agents constantly have the book clubs in mind. Many a manuscript has been tailored with the agent's help for one club or another, occasionally successfully, often unsuccessfully. Perhaps this is done most often with the Dollar Book Club in mind, as that club is perhaps easier to predict than many of the others.

Many of the book clubs object to using a novel which has been condensed for use in an issue of a magazine. Too many of the book club subscribers may have read the story in its condensed form and hence not want to buy the book. If a magazine wishes to buy a book for one number use, the agent or author has to make a choice. In order to obtain a Dollar Book Club selection, an agent recently declined an offer from *Cosmopolitan* to buy a novel for $4,000 for use in one number. The reverse also occurs. Several book club sales have been lost because the agent or author accepted a magazine sale.

Every author of a novel or of a non-fiction book of general interest has a chance for the book club prize, major or minor. The well-known author has the best chance, but many a book by a well-known author does not get tapped. In 1965, there were some fifty titles selected by one or more of the three major book clubs. Nearly half of these were written by relatively unknown authors and four were first novels.

CHAPTER 5 ‖ THE MAGAZINE MARKET

SINCE writing a book is a long and arduous task, most writers start their writing careers by doing short pieces for the magazines. There are seventeen magazines of national circulation which pay top prices for work of free-lance writers: *Cosmopolitan, Esquire, Good Housekeeping, Holiday, Ladies' Home Journal, Life, Look, McCall's, National Geographic, The New Yorker, Playboy, Reader's Digest, Redbook, Saturday Evening Post, Sports Illustrated, True,* and *Woman's Day.* These seventeen magazines in 1966 bought some two thousand articles, some three hundred fifty short stories, a few novelettes and fiction serials, and innumerable jokes, filler material, poems, cartoons, etc.

Payment to the author of an article or of a short story depended upon length, upon the quality of the material and of the writing, and upon whether the author's name was known. Some of these magazines have a policy of paying more than the others. Some pieces were purchased for as little as $500, most for $1,000 or more. A considerable number of authors received several thousands of dollars for a piece. The total outlay to authors from these markets in 1966 was in excess of six million dollars. Eight hundred men and women were contributors, of whom perhaps two hundred earned their livelihood working full time as professional writers. The remaining contributors were newspaper men, housewives, or specialists in some subject who added to their income by selling an occasional piece. Some were book writers who sold part of a book to a magazine. Half of the material in most of these magazines was staff-written, that is, the pieces were written in the office by writers working on a weekly salary. Many of these staff writers are former free-lance writers who prefer the security of a regular wage.

Aside from these seventeen major markets, there are innumerable minor markets. *The Writer's Handbook* (published by The Writer, Inc.) lists over two thousand markets. A dozen of these minor markets pay reasonably well—$250 to $500 for a piece, occasionally more. The great mass of these markets pay under $250, and, in many cases, little more than pin money. Even the most assiduous and successful contributors cannot make a living wage writing for such markets.

The competition to get into the top magazines is severe. *McCall's* alone receives over one thousand manuscripts each week. About 1 per cent of the manuscripts submitted to *McCall's* are purchased. New writers do sell to top markets all the time, but percentage-wise, the chances of any one new writer breaking in is extremely slim. In the minor markets, there is competition, but it is nowhere near as great. More than one thousand new writers break into the minor markets each year.

The editorial staff of a top magazine consists of a top editor, three or more assistant editors, a group of staff readers, and secretarial help. Most magazines have numerous titles for assistants such as managing editor, fiction editor, etc. *McCall's* has fifty-four people doing editorial work; the *Reader's Digest* has over eighty-four. The editor-in-chief usually reads everything before purchase but he probably doesn't spend one-fourth of his time reading. He must approve the magazine cover, all art work, titles of stories and their blurbs, the choice of particular pieces for any one issue, and the order of their appearance in the issue. He must also approve the prices paid to writers and illustrators. He must talk to and write to important authors and confer with executives of the company as to advertising and circulation problems. Likewise the assistant editors have many duties other than reading and rendering opinions. Every manuscript purchased must be proofread, edited, often cut to fit space requirements or for improvement, checked for libel, for good taste, and for anything that may offend a minority group or an advertiser. A character may take a drink of whisky or light a cigarette in a fiction story, but he may not drink Four Roses or light a Chesterfield without offending the makers of other brands of whisky or cigarettes. If the word "Negro" is not capitalized, hundreds of readers will be offended.

It is obviously impossible for the editor to read personally even one-fiftieth of the manuscripts submitted. But every one is read by an assistant editor or staff reader. Every word in the story may not be read. As one famous editor put it, you don't have to eat all of a rotten egg to know that it is rotten. If the manuscript has any real possibilities, it will be read by several people. If they concur that the piece is up to the magazine's standards and possibly suitable for publication, it is placed upon the editor's desk for his final decision of purchase or rejection. It is about as unlikely that a first-class manuscript will be summarily rejected with only one reading as it is that the editor will buy an illiterate one. It has been a tradition with the national magazines that any individual can have his manuscripts read and considered free of charge.

An editor worth his salt is not influenced in his choice of manuscripts by friends, by the advice of an agent or another author, or by the recommendation of an advertiser. In the case of most of the top magazines a close friend of the president of the company would have no better chance of selling a piece to the editor than some unknown writer. Likewise, a big name does not influence the editor if the piece is below standard. Editors often solicit manuscripts from authors with big reputations because such authors are apt to write successful stories and because a well-known name on an effective story may help circulation. But when making the decision to purchase, the editor tries to acquire those pieces which in his judgment are best for his magazine regardless of who wrote them.

Every editor has to keep in mind the formula, the editorial concept, which gives his magazine individuality. The *New Yorker* is as different from the *Reader's Digest* as the sun from the moon. A subscriber to the *New Yorker* does not know what the next issue will contain, but he knows the reading matter will be in the same vein as the previous issue. The same would be true for the *Digest* or any magazine. An editor buys the best manuscripts he can find which fit his editorial concept.

A magazine cannot offend the beliefs of any section of its readers. A magazine cannot now run a story in which a Negro is a humorous or superstitious character, such as occurred in the stories of Octavus Roy Cohen thirty-five years ago. Negro readers do not necessarily object to such stories; white liberal readers usually do. A mass-circulation magazine cannot favor vivisection; there are too many animal lovers who get aroused. Taboos have always restricted the editorial contents of a magazine, but in recent years they have become more prevalent, with a somewhat stultifying effect.

At first blush it seems as if editing a magazine ought to be easy. Every reader thinks he can recognize a good story or an interesting article. Actually, the ability to judge manuscripts successfully requires much experience and knowledge, plus a sixth sense or flair for what pleases the public. Occasionally editors have tried giving their secretarial staff manuscripts to read, but such experiments have not worked satisfactorily. The average person cannot put aside his prejudices and look at a manuscript impersonally, cannot determine whether a particular manuscript does or does not raise his emotional pulse, or whether it will or will not do that to the public at large. Likewise group editing, that is to say a group of editors reading and the majority vote deciding, seldom seems to work satisfactorily.

The editors of the large national magazines are paid somewhere between $50,000 and $100,000 a year. *Cosmopolitan* and *Woman's Day* are both edited by women; the other fifteen are edited by men.

Top editors are men of affairs with catholic tastes. They hold positions of influence. They know or soon become acquainted with many of the leaders in business, labor, government, and the arts. At the same time they must retain the common touch so that their likes and dislikes coincide with those of the great mass of their readers. Successful newspapermen often become good editors; successful writers or novelists are less likely to work out well as editors.

In spite of the prominence and influence of the editor, his position is often insecure. He sits in an uneasy chair. If a magazine begins to lose circulation or advertising, especially if its loss is relatively greater than that of its competitors, the editor is apt to be replaced. There are many living ex-editors. In most cases they lost their positions because they were not sufficiently successful in the eyes of their bosses, the magazine publishers.

The success of an outstanding editor is obvious to all. A man who can invent a successful editorial concept, execute it well, and gradually change the concept as public taste and interest changes, is an editorial genius. DeWitt Wallace started the *Reader's Digest* with a few thousand dollars' capital in 1921. Acting always as his own editor, he has run the circulation up to over sixteen million. When Cyrus H. K. Curtis, founder of the Curtis Publishing Company and publisher of *The Saturday Evening Post,* was asked the secret of his success, he replied: "I can answer that question in three words, George Horace Lorimer." Mr. Lorimer was the editor of the *Post* from

1899, when its circulation was sixteen hundred, to 1937, when its circulation was over three million.

In an attempt to make editing more scientific, many of the popular magazines make use of a service called a survey. The magazine wants to find out the percentage of its readers who read any particular piece, and further whether such readers like the piece. These surveys, although done in different forms, consist basically of asking a representative group of readers what they read and what they liked or disliked. Most editors maintain that these surveys are of value to them only to the extent that they indicate trends in popular taste. For instance, one or more surveys may show an increasing interest in the how-to-do-it-around-the-house pieces and a decreasing interest in foreign affairs or vice-versa.

An author who has had one or more pieces in a popular magazine receives little evidence of popular acclaim. Letters do not flow in. Unless the article contains some stupid mistake, a fan mail of five letters is perhaps average. Likewise, the public forgets or perhaps never remembers the names of the authors. A person will read the *Reader's Digest* from cover to cover and not remember the name of one of the authors of the thirty pieces he had read. Occasionally, an article in a magazine will make a hit and be talked about a great deal, but even then the author's name may not be associated with the piece.

The standard of ethics on the part of the magazines of national circulation is high in contrast to nearly every other medium that uses a writer's material. National magazines have a minimum price for material purchased. The fact that a new author might cheerfully accept anything in order to make a sale and get his manuscript published makes no difference. The magazine insists upon paying its minimum price. No editor takes advantage of an author, whether the author possesses an agent or not. Paying something to an editor personally to promote a sale is unheard of.

National magazines do not attempt to share in the return

from other rights such as motion picture rights. This is refreshing compared to the attitude of many book publishers. The one important exception to this is that nearly all the magazines permit the *Reader's Digest* to reprint their articles for a substantial fee. It is hard to be too critical of the national magazines for not turning over their *Digest* revenue to the author, because the *Digest* itself insists upon paying the author a large reprint fee in addition to the fee paid to the magazine of origin.

An author of a fiction piece should write his story as well as he can, and then submit it to an editor. There is little point in discussing the idea or plot in advance; in fact, there may be harm in doing so. The biggest factor in the case of a fiction story is how well it is done, and no one can have an opinion about that until the finished work can be read.

In the case of non-fiction the situation is different. Here an author should query an editor in advance before writing the article. He should prepare an outline or letter of from three to twelve paragraphs. It should not be a sales talk arguing how good the idea is. The editor can judge that for himself. It should describe the piece the author wants to write, honestly and clearly.

On the basis of an outline, editors will say no or give the author an assignment. This giving an assignment means that the editors like the idea and will hold the subject for the author. If the completed piece does not come off, the editors will try to make suggestions for revision. They will try to buy. Certain editors are rather arbitrary and their approval of an outline does not mean too much.

In the case of a first-class writer, an editor may commission an article, which means he will pay for the piece, whether acceptable or not. At first glance this would seem to be an enviable position for an author to be in. However, if the finished products do not satisfy the editor, the author soon loses this position. Many authors pay little attention to a commission because they know that in the end they must satisfy the editor. The *Reader's Digest* will make a $250 commitment when it gives an assignment. This means the author receives $250 if the completed piece is rejected, and the agreed-upon price, $1,000 or more, if the piece is purchased. An author is free to sell a rejected piece elsewhere. Unless an author has become a regular *Digest* contributor or is dealing with the top echelon or with DeWitt Wallace, a commitment does not mean more than a fifty-fifty chance of ultimate sale, perhaps not even that.

The hazards of the article writer are many. In order to prepare an outline, an author must not only find an idea that seems fresh but he must do some preliminary research work. If the outline fails to bring an assignment, this work is for naught. If the author receives an assignment, he may then find that there really isn't enough material or that the facts do not substantiate his idea. Or it may be that the information depends upon one individual who refuses to see him (this rarely happens) or the individual may refuse to talk except in generalities (this happens more frequently). In such cases the article may blow up.

There are writers who make $25,000 to $40,000 a year from articles, but they are few in number and the road is hard. As the author gets older, he often finds that traveling and the research work become burdensome. Unconsciously he may slight the reportorial side and not gather all the facts and ideas necessary. His articles seem thin and he gets into trouble with his markets. Such a writer had certainly better change to the more sedentary life of writing non-fiction books. In fact, any article writer is well advised to move into books for part of his writing time.

A perennial complaint of authors is the amount of time taken by editors to decide about manuscripts. In the case of a short story, the average magazine takes from two to three weeks to say "no" and a longer period of time to say "yes" on a manuscript it is seriously considering. Certain authors and the leading literary agents get a little quicker action but still the time taken is all too long. As it is an unwritten but well-observed rule that a story should not be offered to two markets at the same time, an author may need as much as six months to circulate his story. All this waiting is extremely irksome to writers. Some fiction and most articles have a timely element; hence delay may kill the value of a manuscript.

Authors have suggested as a remedy for editorial delays that multiple submissions should become the custom, that is, that more than one magazine should be offered the same story at the same time. It is a moot point whether such procedure would be helpful. It might bring worse evils. It might end the present situation in which every author can obtain a reading of his manuscript without benefit of agent. In Hollywood, where multiple submissions are the rule, nearly everything must go through an agent. At any rate, it is unlikely that multiple submissions will become widespread in the magazine field. Many authors tailor their stories to a particular magazine, and work closely with individual editors. Such authors would hesitate to give this up for the doubtful benefits of multiple submissions. However, the slowness of decision does neither author nor editor any good. The Authors League might well look into methods of reducing the delay.

The top magazines are often criticized for taking unwarranted liberties with the author's script after purchase. Magazines rarely send authors proofs of their manuscripts for approval before publication, so that if liberties are taken with an author's script, he does not know it until the piece is in print, when it is too late for him to do anything about it. In respect to editorial changes, nearly all the magazines must plead guilty as far as cutting is concerned. A considerable number of stories and articles are cut by editors because of space requirements. They are physically just too long. The editor feels that he must have a stipulated number of short stories and articles in each issue, and these he must cram into a limited space. Hence cutting is necessary. Other manuscripts will be cut to make them sharper, and, from the editor's point of view, better. (Many authors do overwrite, and therefore such cutting is to the advantage of both buyer and seller.) The *Reader's Digest* cuts, and to a certain extent, rewrites every manuscript it purchases. It does this not merely to sharpen the manuscript, but to get the piece into the *Digest* style.

Theoretically, it would be best if authors cut their own pieces, but authors often are not available, usually hate to cut their own writings, and sometimes do it very poorly. Also, a large number of them do not seem to care whether or not their material is cut or how it is done. Some magazines cut or rather chop out paragraphs at the last minute, usually to make room for a late advertisement just received. In fact, occasionally stories are published in a form so mangled that it is doubtful if the editor would ever have bought them had he considered them in this final version. Authors have every right to complain vigorously as well as take stronger action when this occurs, and it is to be regretted that they so often just seem complacent about the situation. Changing an article deliberately so that the meaning or point of view is altered without the author's full consent practically never occurs. Of course, any such practice would be indefensible.

By custom, an author of a book has the final say as to the title of his own work. In the magazine world, the editor has the final say. Magazine editors are continually changing the titles the authors have chosen for their articles and stories. Recently an author sold *Redbook* a short story, and the editors promptly put on their own title. The title on the published version of a story legally belongs to the author whether it is the author's creation or not. A motion picture company offered $750, not for the story (they did not want the story), but just for the title used in the magazine. The offer was accepted. The author received and kept this motion picture money with the full consent and approval of the editors.

Life, Look, and *The Saturday Evening Post* are fierce competitors. So are the three big women's magazines. For a non-fiction book which seems to have enormous appeal, one of these magazines may pay $100,000 or more. *Look* paid $650,000 for *The Death of a President* by William Manchester, the highest price recorded to date. A magazine which purchases the right to serialize a book will cut or take extracts so as to get three or four articles of five to fifteen thousand words each which will be published in consecutive issues. An agent may offer such material simultaneously to these markets and accept the highest bidder. Often these magazines will contract in advance for a book. An author like Theodore White or William Shirer can tell an editor his plans for his next book and receive a legal contract with money paid upon signing and further money paid upon delivery of the finished book. The same competition and at times competitive bidding exists among *McCall's, Ladies' Home Journal,* and *Good Housekeeping.*

However, the average professional article writer cannot obtain large prices. There are too many writers, too many articles, and seldom is any one article a must for any one magazine. If the writer wants more than perhaps $2,000, the editor can pass up the piece, knowing that he can get as good a piece from someone else at the $2,000 price. The name of the average article writer is not remembered by the public even though it may have appeared as a by-line in the magazine a dozen times. The author has no name, no public following, to sell to the magazine editor. He has only his skill, and no matter how skillful he is, there are many others with about the same skill. He has little or no bargaining power.

The Whites and the Shirers have great bargaining power because their books have given them a name and a public following. A man like MacKinlay Kantor can obtain $5,000 or more for one short article because of his name. His skill may not be any greater than hundreds of others, but his name gives him bargaining power.

Writing magazine articles for a living is tough. Trying to make a living writing magazine fiction is even tougher. In the 1930's and 1940's there was an enormous magazine market for fiction. The *Saturday Evening Post* purchased two hundred or more short stories each year, plus novelettes and some twenty serials. *Collier's* (which suspended publication in 1956) did likewise. The *American Magazine,* which also suspended publication, accounted for another one hundred. There were six women's magazines and many other markets whose main fare for their readers was fiction. This glory for the short story writer has disappeared.

For some inexplicable reason the public's interest in fiction, especially short stories, has faded. One hundred and fifty years ago poetry had an enormous vogue. There occurred an inexplicable change in the reading habits of the public. Today, thousands of people write poetry, but the number of readers (chiefly the poets themselves) is not large. Interest in fiction has not slipped nearly as much as did interest in poetry in the last century, but it has declined and it is probably still declining. Today the number of stories in the popular magazines is scarcely one-tenth of what it was thirty or forty years ago. Moreover, most of the writers who sell a short story to one of the popular magazines find it difficult to repeat. They cannot somehow seem to sell regularly. There are less than a dozen writers who make as much as $10,000 a year writing short stories.

Traditionally, the novelist often learned his trade as a fictioneer by writing and selling short stories to magazines. Today the shrunken magazine fiction market offers little encouragement to the new writer. In non-fiction, the market is still flourishing. The innumerable minor markets—and sometimes the major markets—provide an outlet for the relatively new writer. One can make a good living writing magazine non-fiction or one can use the magazines as a training ground leading to the writing of non-fiction books.

CHAPTER 6 ‖ THE PLAY

THE legitimate theatre gives work to fewer writers than any other great writers' medium. Success here requires maximum ability and superb technical skill. The field is the toughest of any for an author to break into. It abounds in disappointments and failures. There are perhaps one hundred dramatists who would be considered professionals, of which perhaps twenty-five make a living from the stage.

Theatres around Times Square in New York City, located below 54th Street and above 41st, on side streets not far from the avenue called Broadway, are referred to collectively as Broadway. In these theatres during the 1965-66 season, thirty-six dramas and fifteen musicals opened. Revivals of old plays and continued showings of successful plays which opened in previous seasons are not included in these figures. Of these fifty-one shows, thirty-five were failures. Twenty-seven closed after playing for from two or three days to a maximum of ten or twelve weeks. Another eight shows not included in the twenty-seven never had a first night on Broadway; they closed during tryouts outside of New York or after a preview. The backers of these thirty-five failures lost some or all of their money. The authors of the failures made from $1,000 to $4,000 or $5,000, with almost no prospect of making any further income from subsidiary rights. In contrast to these thirty-five failures, there were sixteen enormous successes. The backers of these hits made a profit on their investment of 50 per cent to several hundred per cent. The authors of these hits received from $50,000 to several hundred thousand dollars. Every week, a hit play may make the author $3,000 or $4,000—and a hit play may run for one or more years.

In the case of a hit, often there is substantial money from subsidiary rights. The play may earn for the author a further 20 per cent to 100 per cent of its Broadway revenue playing outside New York City. It also may make money in London, or on the Continent. The amateur rights may be of great value. The play may be sold to the movies at a price ranging from $100,000 to several million dollars, of which the authors would normally get 60 per cent. Half of the 1965-66 hits were sold to motion pictures as of June 1966, and further sales will be made.

The financial return from the book business follows the expected norm. There are an enormous number of books which do not earn the authors more than $3,000, a large number which earn the authors $3,000 to $10,000, a substantial number which earn the authors from $10,000 to $50,000. Finally, maybe one hundred writers earn substantially over $50,000 from royalties and other rights to a book.

The theatre is different. Of those playwrights who in any one season have a Broadway production, about one-third average over $75,000. The others make a modest or microscopic sum. A dramatist is playing for the big stakes. If he misses, his return is almost nil.

Broadway is primarily a world of men. There are three or four women directors and perhaps the same number of women producers. At least four out of five successful dramatists are men. Successful dramatists usually are people who have had long experience in the theatre. There have been many best-selling novels by authors who have had little published previously. The mass-circulation magazines publish many a short piece which is the author's first appearance in print. Similar cases have happened on Broadway, but they are extremely unusual. Successful dramatists nearly always have had much experience in writing, and usually have acquired a knowledge and "feel" for the theatre.

An average play runs to eighteen thousand words. It must hold the audience in rapt attention every minute of the sitting. The lines can never lag. A few sentences of poor dialogue are fatal. This calls for a perfectly finished, highly polished product. All good writing is rewriting, but dramatists probably do more rewriting than any other writers. A play is rewritten and rewritten to satisfy the dramatist himself, and then continually changed and rewritten to fit the cast and satisfy the director and the producer. The script is subject to change right up to the dress rehearsal. The novel can have its weak spots, be overwritten or crudely conceived, and still be successful. Its length (four to twenty times that of the play) leaves plenty of room for verbosity. Readers can skip dull parts. Readers can stop reading—and then resume or not resume. The reader of a novel does not have to wait for the final curtain. Also, many books are bought to be given away as presents and the recipient may never read the gift.

Of the fifty-one new American shows produced on Broadway during the 1965-66 season, ten were dramatizations of novels. In these ten cases the dramatist had to obtain permission and negotiate a contract with the novelist as to distribution of income from the play. A fifty-fifty split of the play's income is the most common division. However a prominent dramatist adapting an obscure novel would usually receive more than 50 per cent. Income from the play includes not only Broadway royalties but receipts from the sale of motion picture and other subsidiary rights. Theoretically, the motion picture rights of the novel could belong to the novelist and the motion picture rights to the play could belong to the dramatist. This would imply two pictures. Actually, the two motion pictures would be too much alike. The Tweedledum picture based upon the novel would be too similar to the Tweedledee picture based upon the play. Hence the motion picture rights to the novel and the play have to be merged into one property and the novelist and the dramatist divide up the receipts from the sale of the motion picture rights of the combined property.

If a musical is adapted from a book, there are usually four parties to share the receipts: the author of the novel, the dramatist, the author of the lyrics, and the composer of the music. If the parties decide to divide up equally, each one would receive one-fourth of the musical's total income.

The play business is a disorganized industry compared to any other writers' medium. There are only a handful of producers like David Merrick who, year in and year out, maintain a permanent staff to consider and produce plays—and even such producers may use outside financing. A large number of producers put on a show now and then, depending upon whether they receive a script they like, and depending upon whether they can obtain the financial backing.

It costs from $100,000 to $200,000 to produce the average drama. For the average musical, the cost range is from $400,000 to $500,000. A drama must run at least ten weeks to break even; a musical, from twenty-five to thirty-five weeks or even longer.

The most curious thing to the outsider is why Broadway produces so many failures. Certainly a book publisher who had Broadway's batting average would soon be out of business. One explanation for the number of atrocious shows to reach Broadway is the difficulty of stopping production once the money is raised. Fifty or more contributors have put up the money, often in lots of from $1,000 to $2,000. Usually, they have read and liked the play. Many of them are suckers who want to gamble. Some of them like the status of being a play backer, and enjoy the opportunity of going to the first-night opening. After some of the money has been spent, the management may discover that the play will not act well, cannot be cast well. The play was exciting to read but cannot be made exciting when staged. Failure seems inevitable but the management has little inducement to kill the show, thereby saving the backers part of their money. Psychologically, it is hard for the management not to continue. The management originally believed in the show and told the backers so. The backers believe in the show and want to see it tested before audiences. The backers do not want to take a partial loss. They hope for profits, and profits are impossible without a production. Also, the management knows that remote as success may seem, still success is always possible. Hence all the money is spent, the play is tested with live actors fully rehearsed, and another failure is chalked up on Broadway.

There is another world of plays in New York City which is called "Off Broadway". The theatre for such plays may be in Greenwich Village or almost anywhere in the city. Often the plays produced are experimental or off-trail. They may give valuable training and experience to authors, actors, and stage designers. Anyone employed here may have a chance to learn to do nearly anything connected with the theatre. In the 1965-66 season, seventy plays were produced Off Broadway.

About $25,000 to $35,000 will finance an Off Broadway production. Stage, sets, and everything else are done on a shoestring. Actors Equity, The Dramatists Guild, and unions have found it impossible to enforce their wage scales and other requirements. "Feather bedding"—requiring that unnecessary employees be hired, etc.—which is so prevalent on Broadway, is non-existent here.

There have been Off Broadway successes. A simple little musical play, *The Fantasticks,* opened in 1960 and is still playing in 1967 to a full house, a house which seats 159 people. The backers have already received $13.50 for each dollar invested, and the authors—miserably paid compared to Broadway—have shared some $50 to $100 a week ever since the opening. Another Off Broadway production, *The Three Penny Opera,* has had a somewhat similar record.

Despite the above, forty-nine out of fifty Off Broadway productions produce little revenue for the dramatist. As the theatre rarely seats more than three hundred and may not even seat one hundred and fifty, box office receipts are small and royalties based upon them are small. An Off Broadway play usually has a short run; one reason is that it does not attract many out-of-town visitors.

There is nothing new about Off Broadway, but only in the last fifteen years or so has it become active enough in the public eye to be important. The theatre traditionally started in Bohemian circles. On Broadway, costs have skyrocketed. There everything becomes a matter of money, and the number of shows produced is small compared to former times. Perhaps the hope of the future is Off Broadway. Perhaps the Off Broadway producers will become financially more reliable. Perhaps authors, actors, and employees will be treated more fairly, at the same time without letting unions and rules hamstring the operation. Perhaps Off Broadway presents a basis for a revival in the American theatre.

When a dramatist writes a play or a script for a musical he usually takes it to a play broker, that is, an agent who specializes in the handling of plays. Occasionally a successful dramatist may produce his own play—in which case he dispenses with a middleman. Some dramatists use theatre lawyers to act as their agents on a fee basis. Occasionally a play is handled by a literary agent. Approximately four-fifths of the plays which opened on Broadway during the 1965-66 season were handled by play brokers or agents, although in many cases only one of the several authors involved was represented by a broker.

When a broker receives a play he likes, he is apt to suggest revision. At times, he may work editorially on the play with the dramatist. The broker then tries to interest a producer. It is customary for him to show a copy of the script to more than one producer at the same time. He may also give a copy to an actor or director. If a leading star or a first-class director is interested in the script, it is much easier to interest a top-ranking producer. It may take a month or two years before a producer is found who thinks he wants to produce a play. The time period is apt to be even longer in the case of a musical. If a producer wants to go ahead, he does not buy the rights to the script the way a publisher buys the rights to a book manuscript. What the producer does is to buy an option to produce within a specified time—perhaps a year or longer. The problems of raising the money, of getting the right cast, or even of getting a theatre, are too great for any producer to obligate himself in advance to produce the play in question. So great are the difficulties that only one out of four plays for which a producer has signed an option contract ever reaches Broadway. The rights to the other three revert to the author. Such an author has received from $500 to $2,000 or more in payment for the option. This money he retains as he starts all over again the weary search for another producer.

Contracts for the sale of plays and musicals on Broadway are controlled by the Dramatists Guild. The Guild is a powerful omnipresent trade association or union. No author can have a play on Broadway unless he has joined the Guild, and signed the Guild agreement so that he agrees to abide by the conditions and terms for authors which the Guild insists upon. Every contract between author and producer becomes valid only when it has been approved and countersigned by the Guild. The following are the most important terms which the Guild's basic minimum production contract requires in the case of every Broadway production.

1. When a producer options a play, he must produce within twelve months or lose his rights. He must pay a minimum advance of $200 a month for the first three months (or $500 for three months if paid at the beginning of the first month). He must pay a minimum of $100 a month for the next three months and $200 a

month for the final six months. Any time the producer
fails to make a monthly payment, he loses his rights.
Once the play opens the monthly payments cease, and
what has already been paid becomes an advance against
royalties.

2. The producer must pay the following minimum royalties: 5 per cent on the first $5,000 of the gross weekly
box office receipts; 7½ per cent of the next $2,000, and
10 per cent thereafter. In lieu of royalties the parties
may agree that the author shall receive 25 per cent of
the weekly operating profits.

3. The producer may not have an interest in the motion
picture or other additional rights to the play of more
than 40 per cent.

4. No changes may be made in the script without the author's permission.

5. The selection of the director and of the cast is subject
to the author's approval.

This is an oversimplification of a long and complicated contract. Any author interested should study the contract and
consult the Guild.

Advances are usually the Guild minimum. These must be
paid to the Guild, and the Guild distributes them to the authors
and the agent. Although advances of $5,000 or more have been
paid, any such sum is rare. The leading dramatists are working for the big prize of a long run and enormous royalties. The
new or little-known playwright cannot command a high advance.

The Guild's minimum terms have become, to a great extent, the maximum terms paid. Although a few leading dramatists receive a royalty up to 15 per cent, the great mass of contracts stipulate the Guild minimum royalty. With respect to
motion picture rights, it is practically unheard of for the playwright to receive more than 60 per cent.

Just as the Guild must countersign any contract for play
production on Broadway, so it must approve any contract for
the sale of the picture rights. The Guild lawyer, acting under

the title of arbiter, takes an active part in the negotiations for the sale of the picture rights. The Guild collects the money and pays the authors, the management, and the agent. The salary of the arbiter is paid under Guild rules from part of the agent's commission or, if there is no agent, from part of the author's royalty.

The power given the dramatist by the Guild over both changes in the script and the selection of the director and cast is important. The director or producer may have many suggestions, but the author's decision is final. The author usually attends rehearsals so that he can change the script as a result of watching how the lines "go over" when spoken.

When a play reaches Broadway there is an official opening night which the drama critics attend to review the play for the press and for radio and television. These play reviewers are better paid and more competent than most book reviewers. Book reviewers give valuable publicity to the book industry; they rarely affect the sale of an individual book substantially, they rarely make or break a book. The drama critics have extraordinary power and influence. In a large number of cases, they make or break a play. There is no evidence of favoritism. Critics shun dramatists, producers, and brokers, and it is unknown for any playwright to have an "in" or "pull" or influence with a critic.

Smash hit plays, especially musicals, have in general brought higher sums in Hollywood than has been the case with the leading best-selling novels. *My Fair Lady* was sold for five and one-half million dollars and this sum was an advance against an interest for the authors in the picture (the equivalent of a royalty). The authors have already collected eight million dollars over and above the advance.

At first blush, it might seem curious that a smash hit play or musical should be more valuable in pictures than a leading best-selling novel. The nationwide publicity of a best seller exceeds the publicity of a smash hit on Broadway. The number of people who read a successful novel exceeds the number of people who view a hit play. One must take into consideration that there are several readers of a novel for every copy purchased in a bookstore and probably twenty or more readers for every copy purchased by a library. Furthermore there is book club readership, plus the millions who may read the paperback. Nevertheless, plays have brought the higher sums from Hollywood. There are various reasons for this. In the first place, the play or musical and the picture media are close; the novel is a thing apart. A good play or musical, because of its form, is more likely to make a good picture than many a novel. Secondly, the play can often be turned into a relatively inexpensive picture. After all, a play's stage sets are limited while, for example, a historical novel may wander all over the world with an enormous cast and much pageantry which is expensive to shoot.

The standard of ethics for show business is not as high as that of the more stabilized media such as book or magazine publishing, but it is higher than one would expect. Leading producers such as David Merrick or Jean Dalrymple are absolutely reliable and their word would be good without question. However, there are minor producers on the fringe of the industry who cannot be trusted. One producer who had had a previous show on Broadway gave a bad check as an advance option for a musical. This is not typical; the curious thing is that it happened at all.

With two or three exceptions the leading play brokers are connected with large Hollywood-oriented agencies who represent actors, directors, producers, and maybe even bands as well as playwrights. Representing authors of plays is a small part of their business. William Morris and Ashley Famous Agency are in this category. When such a broker tries to sell a play, there is a danger that he may try to sell with it an actor or director. Perhaps he offers a package deal. He may truly believe that his actor-client is best for the part but his judgment is influenced by the fact that the actor is his client. It is difficult for the dramatist to deal with this situation. He may not be aware of it until too late. He tends anyway to follow the advice of his broker. The broker handling talent may argue that he is in a better position to sell the play or cooperate in obtaining a good cast because of his talent clients. This argument has doubtful value. The broker is involved in a conflict of interest and getting the best setup for the play may be subordinate to placing his talent.

The good broker should have the qualifications of a literary agent as well as a large acquaintance among producers, directors, and stars. He should know the theatre almost to the extent of having lived and slept in it. Judgment is important. So is the ability to be persuasive and to work out compromises among producer, director and stars—always with the author's interest in view. Occasionally a literary agent or a Hollywood agent who lacks a New York office specializing in the theatre will handle a play. As a rule, neither of these is capable of doing the job properly. The good broker is in no hurry to have a contract signed. This in itself amounts to little except to tie up the rights to the play. The vital concern of the good broker is whether there will be adequate financing, and who the director and possibly even who the stars will be. The percentage of a broker's plays which actually reach Broadway is the test of how good he is.

Dramatists write for Broadway and Off Broadway, but there is another market for plays of a special type, the amateur market. Perhaps fifty to one hundred writers are involved here. The money they take in is a pittance compared to a Broadway hit; it is substantial compared to a Broadway flop or even an Off Broadway hit. Schools, churches, and amateur acting groups put on these plays. It has been estimated that there are some twenty-five thousand amateur groups in the country, of which perhaps some ten thousand pay for the rights to one or more plays a year.

Several firms of substantial size do this business—perhaps The Dramatic Publishing Company, Samuel French, and the Dramatists' Play Service are the best known. These firms acquire the rights to a play suitable for amateur production. They then charge from $5 to $50 per performance. They are also in the publishing business, selling paperback copies of the plays at prices ranging from forty cents to a dollar. An amateur group may need twenty or more copies for the director and cast. The remuneration to the dramatist is twofold, a royalty on each performance and a royalty on the sale of each copy of the play as a book. Plays may be one-act or may be full-length, with a playing time of from two to two and one-half hours. Sometimes beginning authors will sell a play outright for as little as fifty dollars instead of making a royalty arrangement.

Plays which have appeared on Broadway are often produced by amateur casts, and perhaps thirty or forty of these plays (mostly handled by the Dramatists Play Service) have brought a return in six figures to the author. However, there is a demand for plays especially written for the amateur market. Sets must be simple, roles not too difficult to act, the roles of the stars not too prominent, and so on. Above all, schools and churches must have a clean play. Broadway hits, even if they have the other requirements, are often too spicy, with dialogue not appropriate for children, churches, or small-town audiences.

The plays for this market may be originals or may be adaptations of novels. *The Bishop's Mantle* by Agnes Sligh Turnbull has been successfully dramatized for this market. Likewise one episode from the Pulitzer Prize-winning novel, *The Town,* by Conrad Richter made a good one-act play for amateurs.

A successful play in this field may be performed for a long period of time. There have been a few that have earned as much as $30,000 to $40,000. The average return may be $1,000 to $3,000 for a full-length play, less for a one-act play.

Certain writers sell half a dozen such plays a year. This is a logical market for the beginner who is ambitious to become a successful dramatist. There is nothing easy in the word business. This market is not easy, but it does not present the overwhelming obstacles which must be faced on Broadway.

Despite the difficulties and the gamble, the playwrights who write successfully for Broadway are more contented than are writers in any other medium. The author of a flop is, of course, disappointed, often terribly so, but he has no one to blame except the weakness of his own script and the public taste. He has signed with the individual producer. He has approved the director and the cast. Upon request he may have made many changes in his play, but the decision to make them and the actual working of the revisions have been his own. Even though the author of a flop may be overwhelmed by the blow, he rarely blames his agent or the industry.

There can be no question that today's working conditions for the dramatist are infinitely superior to those of fifty years ago before the development of the Guild's strength. In no sphere of writing were authors treated with such gross unfairness as they were in the theatre in the days of old. Today, because of a strong Guild, their treatment on Broadway could scarcely be better. There is nothing comparable to the frustration of the Hollywood motion picture writer, the bitterness toward the industry of the television writer, the feeling of dissatisfaction with his publisher on the part of many a book author, or the feeling on the part of the mass-circulation magazine writer that he is subject to an arbitrary editorial decision. Of course, the half-successful dramatist or the unsuccessful ones leave the medium, or perhaps it should be said that they never enter it. All the other writers' media are filled with authors twenty or fifty or seventy per cent successful. This situation does not exist on Broadway.

Broadway play producing is in an unhealthy financial situation. Perhaps the cost of a theatre ticket is too high. Certainly the expense of putting on a show seems exorbitant. To a considerable extent this is due to the theatre's being burdened and in some cases hamstrung by the unions. More plays and more musicals would be produced if the unions were less powerful or more reasonable, and there would be more work for everyone, and more royalties for a larger number of dramatists. The Dramatist Guild is a minute factor—if a factor at all—in maintaining the present high cost of theatrical production, and there is probably little it could do about the situation if its members wanted to. If in the book industry 10 to 15 per cent of the gross (retail price) is fair as a royalty, certainly 5 per cent rising to 10 per cent of the gross is not an unfair royalty for dramatists. If the industry is sick, there seems no way that authors can aid it.

It is a pity that the Guild does not insist upon a complete separation between the function of the play broker and the talent agent, but authors seem so devoted to their agents and so unconscious of their frequently diverse interests that this is unlikely to occur in the near future. Doubtless there are other minor matters which could be improved, but to the outsider the dramatist's relation to his trade seems to be as ideal as can be expected in human affairs. What is so remarkable is that this should be the situation in the hectic gambling venture of show business.

CHAPTER 7 ‖ HOLLYWOOD

O_F the seventeen hundred novels published in 1966, about eighty (or 5 per cent) were purchased for motion picture use. A few of these novels were bought for as little as $2,500, and a small number for over $100,000. James Michener received $500,000 for *The Source*. The great majority went for a figure between $10,000 and $100,000. A first novel, *The Dirty Dozen* by E. M. Nathanson, was sold for $80,000.

Of the thousands of non-fiction books published in 1966, only some twenty were sold to motion pictures. Statistically, this meant that a non-fiction author's chance of making a picture sale of a book of general appeal was less than one-half of 1 per cent.

In the case of some of these picture sales, the author not only received the sales price, but he also had an interest in the picture. He may have had a per cent of the producer's profit from the film, or a per cent of the gross earnings. Any such percentage would be small, but if the picture should make a lot of money, the dollar return conceivably could be enormous.

Altogether, therefore, some one hundred authors actually sold the picture rights to their books. There were probably another one hundred authors who made tentative sales, who sold options to buy picture rights. When an author sells an option, he receives an agreed upon down payment—perhaps $2,500. He agrees for a period of time—perhaps twelve months—to keep his motion picture rights available for the purchaser of the option. At the end of the time period, the option purchaser has the right to acquire the motion picture rights by paying the agreed-upon final price—perhaps $25,000. If the option buyer fails to make the final payment, the rights remain with the author and the author is free to dispose of them elsewhere. The dollar figures for options vary widely, and so does the length of time that an option has to run.

When a motion picture producer buys an option, the producer hopes to make the picture based upon the book, but he is by no means sure that he can. He is buying time, perhaps to see if he can raise the capital to finance the picture or perhaps to see whether a screen writer can successfully dramatize the book.

If the motion picture option is exercised, the situation is the same as if the author had made an outright sale except that his remuneration has been delayed. However, four out of five motion picture options never get exercised. Here the outlook for the future is gloomy. The book whose options are not exercised rarely finds a buyer elsewhere. It is too late for a motion picture sale. The book is no longer selling to the public, it is no longer in the public eye. Motion picture buyers are uninterested. The author who sells a motion picture option should not expect the option to be exercised, and he should not expect the book to be sold elsewhere. He should assume that his option money is all that he will ever see.

There are three types of motion picture buyers. There are the large companies such as Metro-Goldwyn-Mayer, Fox Films, Warner Bros., etc. Metro alone makes some forty films a year. These companies make inexpensive films and multi-million-dollar ones. They pay small prices and enormous prices for properties. Second, there are a substantial number of independent producers, each of whom may make from one to three pictures a year. These men have access to ample capital and may buy a book cheaply or pay an enormous price. There

is a third category, a large number of small independent producers with limited access to money. These people move in
and out of the business. Usually they try to buy rights cheaply
and make inexpensive films. They are the great buyers of motion picture options.

How much money a book publisher will advance an author
for his next book is more or less predictable. There is no yard-
stick as to how much can be obtained for the motion picture
rights to a book. When dealing with motion picture buyers, the
author and his agent are engaged in a poker game. The buyer,
of course, has a maximum figure in his mind. Usually, he tries
to keep the combined cost of the book and of the screen play
based upon the book to under 10 per cent of the estimated cost
of the picture. A picture budgeted at $1,000,000 could then
carry $100,000 for the novel and the screen writer—perhaps
$50,000 each. A producer who has only $250,000 to finance a
picture would probably not pay more than $10,000 or $15,000
for the motion picture rights to the novel. However, the seller
often has little way of guessing the estimated cost, and the
buyer is either not telling or else what he says about his plans
cannot be depended upon. When a deal for the sale of a book
to pictures is concluded, the seller never knows whether he
has obtained the maximum money possible. Probably, in many
cases he has not. However, if one tries for the maximum, one
runs the risk of pricing oneself out of the market and never
making a sale. Perhaps a producer is interested in buying a
particular novel, novel X, and his top figure is $25,000. Per-
haps the producer offers as a bargaining price $15,000 or $20,-
000. Naturally, he asserts that this is all he can pay. Perhaps the author and his agent, ignorant of the buyer's top
figure, price the book at $50,000. Then a month later, the
author, wanting to make a sale, drops his price to $25,000. It
is too late. The producer has found and purchased another
novel and is no longer interested in novel X. The author and his
agent inadvertently have priced themselves out of the market.

When a price is agreed upon between the author and a buyer of motion picture rights, the author is presented with a contract, much of which is unintelligible to anyone but a motion picture lawyer. The document will contain from two to five thousand words in small type with a reading time of perhaps one half hour. Various assignments, riders and exhibits may be attached to make the document all the more formidable. The author should watch for the following:

1. The amount of money to be paid to the author and when it is to be paid. In the case of a sale for a large sum, the author may want to spread the money over several years for tax purposes. For instance, a sale at a price of $75,000 might be paid for at the rate of $15,000 a year for five years.

2. Sometimes a deal is made where the author is to receive a lump sum of money and also a percentage of the gross. The gross is the total amount of money that the motion picture company receives for the sale or rental of the picture. It is reasonably easy for an author to collect a per cent of the gross. Sometimes a deal is made where the author is to receive a lump payment and also a per cent of the profits. To define profits satisfactorily so that the author can collect if the picture does make money is a complicated legal affair, and this is one of the reasons an author usually should retain a motion picture lawyer. It is rare under any circumstances for an author to make much money from a per cent of the profits.

3. If a motion picture is successful, a few years later the company may reshoot the picture using actors wearing current fashions, etc. Does the author get further money for a remake? Usually he doesn't. Sometimes a company will make a sequel to the picture—further adventures of the detective in a new picture. Has the company the right to do this, and will the author receive additional money for each sequel?

4. Sometimes the deal includes a clause that the picture buyer is to pay more money if the novel is accepted

by a major book club or if the hardback sale exceeds a certain amount. Perhaps the author is to receive $10,000 extra if there is a major book club selection and perhaps twenty-five cents extra for every copy sold in the hardback edition over fifty thousand copies. This kind of an agreement would occur only if the picture rights to the novel were sold before or around publication time.

5. When a motion picture buyer buys a book for pictures, the buyer always insists on having the right to sell his motion picture or a condensed version of it to television. However, the buyer should not have the right to dramatize the book for a television series without paying the author further money. The contract should be clear on this point.

6. The contract should have a clear clause to the effect that all publication rights belong to the author. The contract will permit the buyer to make a résumé of the picture and of the book in not more than seventy-five hundred words. This résumé may be printed in pamphlet form or given away (never sold) to newspapers and magazines to help promote the picture. This right is universally granted, and, from the point of view of the author, is harmless.

The author should bargain stubbornly over the above six points. He can fairly safely ignore the other multitudinous clauses in the proffered contract. The rest of the contact, which equals the length of a short story, can be considered wordage set down by lawyers to cover remote contingencies.

An author who sells the motion picture rights to his book has no control over the quality of the resulting picture. The picture may follow the story closely or have little relation to the published work. If the novel has had only a moderate sale, the title of the picture may be different from that of the novel. The late Ben Ames Williams once watched a picture and then remarked to his wife that the movie was pretty good —he wondered who had written the story from which the picture was made. They waited for the next showing so that they could see the credits, only to discover that the picture allegedly was based upon one of Williams' own stories.

An author's prestige or literary reputation is not affected by a motion picture. An artistically good picture does not help an author's reputation; an artistically poor picture does not hurt him. A commercially successful picture may increase an author's paperback sales. Aside from this, it has no appreciable effect upon his monetary return. A commercially unsuccessful picture has no adverse effect upon an author's revenue.

When a picture is produced, the name of the author of the book is flashed upon the screen. Theoretically, this should be good publicity for the author. Millions of viewers see the author's name. Actually, this is unimportant. Viewers do not notice or remember the name of the author. It is similar to the exposure that an editor's name receives in a magazine. DeWitt Wallace's name as editor or publisher of *The Reader's Digest* has been on the masthead of every issue of that magazine since 1920. Each month some twenty-five million people all over the world theoretically notice his name. Actually, they do not. It is doubtful if one out of a hundred subscribers to the *Digest* has ever heard of DeWitt Wallace.

There is a big market for the picture rights to books but the market is heavily weighted in favor of the best seller. Three out of four of the top fiction best sellers and perhaps one out of four of the top non-fiction best sellers are sold to pictures. It is for the best sellers that the big prices are usually paid. Of the hundreds of novels which have only moderate sales, scarcely one out of twenty-five reaches the screen. This disparity would be much greater in the case of non-fiction. The prices paid for the non-best sellers are usually moderate. There are three reasons why the best seller is so sought after in Hollywood:

1. The title of a best seller is known to hundreds of thousands of people so that a picture using that title starts

off as a somewhat known product. It is easier for the distributor of the picture to get the picture shown in a large number of motion picture theatres. Large audiences are more likely to come when at least some of the public have heard of the title.

2. The success of the best seller indicates that the public wants to read this author's particular conception. Hence, there is at least an implication that audiences will want to view this particular conception dramatized for the screen.

3. Every producer in the market for motion picture property in the United States has been exposed to the best seller. Producers, directors, actors, and the motion picture industry in general talk about it. When every potential buyer knows about a book, obviously a sale is more likely. The most dedicated agent cannot obtain similar exposure for a moderate seller, for just another novel.

Hollywood pays book authors each year a total sum in excess of six million dollars. Much of this goes to the best-selling authors but still the Hollywood lightning continually strikes some obscure book to the surprise and pleasure of everyone.

CHAPTER 8 ‖ *TELEVISION AND MOTION PICTURE WRITERS*

O_{NLY} occasionally does an author sell his book to the movies or to television. Nevertheless, pictures—and the ever-present television—represent a large medium for writers.

There are some fifteen hundred working motion picture and television writers in Hollywood. Perhaps one hundred of these writers work exclusively for pictures; eight hundred probably work exclusively for television. The others write for pictures when they can, but, more often than not, they work for television. These fifteen hundred writers create more than 90 per cent of the motion picture screen plays and 80 per cent of the television screen plays.

What is writing for Hollywood like? Who are the writers? In the first place, 90 per cent of them are men. Their average age is under forty. A few are former magazine contributors who have found writing for pictures or television more profitable; a few are dramatists who perhaps wrote one Broadway hit but could not repeat—or perhaps wrote one produced play that was a flop; some are former newspaper men; some are old pros who have been working in Hollywood for twenty years or longer. Quite a large number are younger aspirants attracted by the chance to write, by the alleged glamour, and by the possibility of making a lot of money.

About a dozen top screen writers live in New York or its environs and periodically fly across the continent; another dozen live in London; a handful, in Rome; and a few else-where. But Hollywood is the center for motion picture writing, and although television writing is divided between Hollywood and New York, four out of five TV writers work in Holly-wood.

When a writer gets a job in Hollywood he is given what is called an assignment. He agrees in advance to do a specific writing job, and signs a contract that guarantees him the agreed-upon payment. His assignment may be to prepare a mo-tion picture screenplay based upon a published book, a Broad-way play, or an unpublished story, or to rewrite someone else's screenplay. Writing this motion picture screenplay, with revisions, may require six to fifteen or more weeks of work.

In television, an assignment is different. Here the writer is usually paid to prepare a television screenplay based on an idea of his own. The writer describes his idea to a potential buyer, usually a producer or a story editor. If the idea is ap-proved, the writer, for an agreed-upon price, then creates a television screenplay. Writing a half-hour television show usu-ally requires at least two weeks; an hour show, three to four or even five weeks.

Every writer who gets a writing job in Hollywood must join a union, the large and powerful Writers Guild of America East and West. The only exception is the newcomer, the apprentice, who may work on assignment on his first job as a non-union man. Once in the union, a writer caught breaking union rules can be deprived of work indefinitely. A producer who violates the agreement can be blacklisted and prevented from hiring writers.

The Guild negotiates with both the motion picture and tel-evision industry, and contracts are agreed upon between the union on the one hand and the studios and independent pro-ducers on the other. The contract now in force for motion pic-ture writers on assignment stipulates the following minimum payment:

For a motion picture screenplay (twelve
  weeks' work at $375.38 per week)　　　　　$4,504.56

The contract in force to date for all television writers on assignment stipulates the following minimum payments:

Idea and fifteen-minute screenplay	$ 612.61
Idea and thirty-minute screenplay	1,321.32
Idea and sixty-minute screenplay	2,402.40
Idea and ninety-minute screenplay	3,482.96

These minimum payments vary, depending on complicated
factors. A writer gets more when he is working on a high-
budget picture or television show; minimum rates also vary
with the number of weeks guaranteed or worked, with the number of writers on the same assignment, etc.

Guild rules are almost never circumvented, with one exception: The Guild forbids a writer seeking a television assignment to do any speculative writing; when seeking an assignment, he is supposed to tell his story orally. In practice,
the writer does tell his idea, but he also often gives the producer an outline to show his colleagues. Sometimes an outline even will be rewritten at the suggestion of a producer.
The Guild now winks at such violations, and, ultimately, the
rule that forbids outlines may be changed.

Only the beginning or relatively unsuccessful writers receive Guild minimum fees. Four-fifths of the writers receive
more—perhaps one-third receive at least twice as much. However, few writers work all the time. A writer of half-hour
television scripts rarely can dream up and sell twenty ideas a
year. Often, he is lucky to sell ten, which may mean only
twenty to thirty weeks' work a year.

The market for writers rises and falls. In 1965, the most
writers working on assignment in pictures in any one month
was 172, and the low was 125. In television the top was 726,
the low, 370.

The two dozen or so top motion picture writers make enormous incomes. Dan Taradash, for example, obtained an assignment to write a screenplay based upon James Michener's novel, *Hawaii*, and he was paid a quarter of a million dollars. More than a dozen writers get $100,000 or more for an assignment.

Every Hollywood writer prefers to write for pictures rather than for television because pictures pay more. Also, the writer for pictures has more creative freedom. The television writer is "cabined . . . confined." The length of a TV script is arbitrary (it cannot vary even a minute); the small television screen restricts the scenes that can be portrayed; a television show has strict financial limitations; and often the writer must use inexpensive backgrounds, and confine himself to a small cast of characters.

While most screenplays are written on assignment, a certain number are original screenplays—created by authors not writing on assignment or working with producers. These are written on speculation and sold to producers just the way a short story is written and sold to a magazine. There is no Guild minimum for an original screenplay—prices range from as little as $2,500 to more than six figures, with the majority selling in the range of $10,000 to $25,000.

In television it is also theoretically possible to write and sell an original screenplay, called a teleplay. However, only one show has been purchasing original teleplays, and this show bought only a few in the last few months. This situation is changing, and the market for original teleplays may expand in the future.

In the motion picture and television industry, unlike other writers' media, an agent is a necessity. Stars, directors, producers, and writers all have agents, or, in the case of a few top money-makers, an attorney who performs functions similar to the agent's. The agent business may not make much sense in a rational world, but this is beside the point. To the neophyte writer in Hollywood an agent is obligatory. Only through an agent can a writer obtain an assignment. No studio, and few, if any, producers, will consider an unknown writer's script unless it is submitted through an agent.

To the new writer, Hollywood seems the most difficult of all the great writing media to crack. First, there seems to him no way of obtaining an agent. In all probability no agent will look at the new writer's script or consider him for an assignment—the writer either receives a polite no, or his query goes unanswered. The writer may ask for a personal appointment and the agent refuses; the agent is too busy.

With agents remote, aloof, and completely uninterested, the barriers to breaking into Hollywood, then, seem insurmountable. Actually, this is not the case. Every writer's medium is extremely hard to crack; Hollywood is no more difficult than the others. The problem is just different. What steps must the neophyte take?

First, he must learn his trade. Screenplays have been published, and the writer can obtain some to study. Some articles and books on writing for motion pictures and television may be helpful. The neophyte, just for practice, can write and rewrite screenplays, struggling to get better and better.

Second, the neophyte can sometimes work in a local television station, not necessarily as a writer. Any job where at times he can watch the shooting of scripts will be helpful. Experience in a television station will add to his competence, and be a plus to his getting an assignment in Hollywood at some later date.

Third, once the neophyte believes that he has learned his trade he must go to Hollywood. Trying to sell oneself or one's scripts at a distance is a well-nigh hopeless proposition.

Fourth, arriving in Hollywood, the neophyte must talk some agent into reading his scripts, as examples and evidence of the writer's competence. The writer first may talk some producer

or director or writer acquaintance into reading his scripts un-
officially, and then recommending the writer to an agent. Some
neophyte writers barge in cold on person after person until
they find someone who will read their scripts and give them
an introduction to an agent.

Number 4 of the above presupposes a smooth talker. Most
successful Hollywood writers must not only have the competence (the first requirement) but also a glib tongue. If the neophyte is not good at selling himself, if he cannot describe a
story well, he is under a handicap.

To the ordinary workaday writer living in the East, going to
Hollywood to work for a studio is an extraordinary experience. Hollywood is not a town or governmental unit. It is a Post
Office address and a telephone exchange in an outlying part
of Los Angeles. Close by are residential areas such as Beverly
Hills or Brentwood. The temperature is warm and constant,
with little rain. Much of the land is fairly flat, but it is sur-
rounded by mountains, hills, ravines, and canyons, with wind-
ing roads and abrupt climbs, and, often, gorgeous views. In
this area, within a radius of four or five miles, are the Metro,
Fox, Paramount, Columbia, Warner Brothers, Universal, and
the United Artists studios plus NBC, ABC, and CBS, and several other TV studios.

The writer living in this charming locality has ideal physical
working conditions. There is no clock punching; no five-day
work week; no nine-to-five working hours. The writer can
work at home on his own schedule. Ninety per cent of the television writers work at home; motion picture writers more often
work in a studio office (perhaps because office conditions are
so pleasant), but two-thirds of these work at home. Confer-
ences are inevitable, and once or twice a week the writer drives
to the studio to confer with his producer or boss, but such con-
ferences are informal.

Nevertheless the typical Hollywood writer, doing creative
work of a fashion, living in a beautiful atmosphere, boss of his

working hours, is a frustrated, unhappy man. His frustration begins because he is doing creative work, but his producer and others continually instruct him as to how to do it. It is as if a novelist had to devise his characters and his plot according to his publisher's instructions, then deliver his novel to the publisher chapter by chapter, and rewrite each chapter as bidden. Any novelist working under such conditions would be frustrated. The screen writer, required to work this way, lives with frustration.

There are other reasons for a screen writer's unhappiness. A motion picture is not the sole creation of a writer. The effectiveness of the picture depends upon the cast, upon the director, upon the composer (all pictures have some music), and upon the money spent upon sets, etc. The writer of the screenplay may be blamed when the failure of the picture was in no way his fault, or the praise for success may go to some star when the major cause for success was really the writer's. This situation gives any writer a basis for frustration.

Moreover, writers write for prestige as well as for money, and the writer of a screenplay gets almost no credit from the public. It is true that his name is flashed upon the screen as the author of the screenplay, but the public is uninterested. Who goes to a movie and says to himself, "My, what a fine screenplay"? The only people who remember who wrote a specific picture are other writers and members of the industry in Hollywood.

The frustration of the motion picture writer is paralleled by the frustration of the television writer. Every television writer wants to write for pictures. If he occasionally gets motion picture work, he is unhappy when he has to work for TV. If he never is able to get motion picture work, he is all the more unhappy. There are dramas on TV that are good from a critical point of view, but nineteen of twenty are drivel, and the writers know it. There is at least local adulation for the writer of a successful motion picture screenplay; there is little adulation for most TV writers.

Idleness is another cause of the Hollywood writer's frustration. Few writers at the beginning of the year know how many weeks they will work or what their income is likely to be. They do not take vacations from work. Their idleness is interrupted by work.

There is another indirect but possible cause for a Hollywood writer's frustration. A writer on assignment is an employee, but an employee who changes his job a dozen times a year. Hence, he has little sense of loyalty to any studio or any producer, and less chance of making enduring business friendships.

Then there is the problem of living in a community where everything oozes money. In all walks of life people want all the money they can get, even though it is demonstrable that a group of rich people are no happier than a group of moderately rich. In Hollywood, the desire for money is carried to the extreme. Money is Hollywood's life blood, its only standard, its status symbol, the only desideratum.

Everyone talks of money. If a writer is out of work and broke, each of his acquaintances knows it. When a writer is working, his acquaintances know about how much he is getting. A producer boasted to me that he could know within 10 per cent how much money any individual made. He said, "Tell me what a man does in the industry, and where he has last worked, and after a couple of telephone calls I can tell you his income."

In Hollywood, friends are in approximately the same financial bracket. A poorly paid writer (except in the case of long years of friendship) would not be seen lunching with a well-known, successful producer, director, or top writer who gets perhaps $100,000 an assignment.

On one business trip to Hollywood, I was told by a top

screen writer—a woman whose fee for writing a screenplay was in six figures—that she wanted to give a dinner party for me, and was there any particular person I would like to have invited. I suggested a college classmate and close friend who was then writing TV Westerns at the Guild minimum. My hostess said she would be delighted to ask him. The next day she called me in great embarrassment. She told me that she had invited a certain motion picture star, the general manager of one of the studios, and various other well-known Hollywood characters, and that she hoped I would understand that my friend would be uncomfortable, and that she really should not invite him. My hostess had made inquiries and discovered what my friend was making. In point of fact, I was also ineligible for the dinner party on financial grounds, but as I came from New York, no one knew.

Most writers in other media feel frustrated at one time or another. The feeling may be intense, but usually it is temporary. It is a feeling of frustration because the writer cannot reproduce on paper what is in his mind's eye, because a page or a chapter does not seem right. However, few writers of fiction or non-fiction or legitimate drama feel frustrated all the time, or feel frustrated because of the industry. They want to write. They continue to write even though the monetary return may be small, even though they are only partially successful.

The forty or fifty most successful Hollywood writers enjoy the occupation. In a money world they are at the top. They have prestige, at least in their own home town, Hollywood. Because of their names, their positions, their competence, they are given more freedom to write creatively than is the average writer. However, the great mass of Hollywood writers complain about the occupation, the industry, and their frustrations. Their money, whether substantial or not, is never enough in their Hollywood money world.

If the Hollywood writers are frustrated and the non-Hollywood writers are relatively happy, why don't Hollywood writers enter one of the other writers' media? A handful, such as Irving Wallace, have become brilliant novelists. Many try, but usually they are unsuccessful. Writing for the films or TV reduces one's capacity to write good books or to publish in the top magazines.

There are many reasons. The writer for films does not have to show any great depth of characterization. The stars, with the aid of the director, do that. For the film-writer, much is plausible because one sees it happen on the screen. Motivation is less essential. A motion-picture viewer does not question whether a character would leave a room, because the viewer sees him leave. Furthermore, a film-writer rarely does intensive research work, such as is necessary for the non-fiction book and usually desirable even for the modern novel. Then again, a film-writer is dealing in large part with other people's ideas. If he dramatizes a book, he is dealing with the novelist's idea. If he obtains a television assignment, his own idea is tailored to the concept of the TV show.

Finally, the film-writer deals with gimmicks, twists, and dialogue, occasionally just for their own sake. The successful film-writer has acquired great technical skill, great craftsmanship. He has special gifts. But when such a writer tries to be a novelist, he finds it difficult to abandon his film technique. He finds it difficult to show characters in depth, to probe motivations, to immerse himself in research dealing solely with his own ideas, to avoid the gimmicks and twists, the props of a film-writer. Most Hollywood writers have the time to write books. Many have the urge. But when they try, seldom can they shuck off the Hollywood influence.

CHAPTER 9 ‖ THE LITERARY AGENT

WE have discussed the great writers' media and the writers who write for these. There is one occupation so directly related to the writing trade as to warrant a separate chapter. The occupation is that of the literary agent.

Once a month, six men and one woman—seven of the leading literary agents of New York City—lunch together. In business they are rivals, but they are scarcely conscious of the competition. They are close friends who like to exchange news and gossip of the literary market. Collectively, these agents sell in excess of $12,000,000 worth of literary material each year. Collectively, they represent some fifteen hundred writers. Some of their writers are literary figures such as John Dos Passos or Conrad Richter. Other clients may write the so-called non-book. The agents represent enormous money-makers such as Irving Wallace, H. Allen Smith, Daphne Du Maurier, Morris West, William Shirer, and Agatha Christie; and they represent first novelists whose books may sell fewer than twenty-five hundred copies and may earn less than $1,500.

What do these agents do?

The primary function of the literary agent is to obtain for an author as much money as possible. Authors often are not good businessmen: They are poor judges of their own work, and in their modesty they may underrate it, or in their egotism they may overrate it. The agent sells the manuscripts of his clients, negotiates the price and the details of the contract, collects the money from the buyer, retains a 10 per cent commission, and remits 90 per cent to the author. Or, in the case of a book idea with sensationally high sales potential, he may conduct an auction before one word is written. He may offer a dozen copies of the manuscript to a dozen potential buyers, asking for bids (this would be done *only* with a very valuable property by a big name writer). Or he may assiduously offer one manuscript to publisher after publisher. The agent may fail to sell such a manuscript, or may find a buyer only after many declinations. In one case, an agent made a sale only on the sixty-sixth submission.

An agent deals in many rights. He may make a contract with a book publisher for book publication, then another contract with a magazine for first magazine publication, and a third contract for the motion picture or television rights. He also may do a substantial foreign business, making contracts for publication in London and for translation on the Continent. The agent for *The Rise and Fall of the Third Reich,* by William L. Shirer, made more than twenty individual contracts for separate rights to the book. Agents, of course, also handle many short stories and articles and, occasionally, screenplays. Fewer than 5 per cent of the published novels are sold to the movies, but the revenue from such sales may be enormous: An author such as James Michener or Irving Wallace may get a quarter of a million dollars or more for the picture rights to a novel.

The leading New York agents employ from eight to twenty people, including a bookkeeper, an office boy, secretaries, etc. Large agencies are somewhat compartmentalized: One person may handle nothing but translation rights, and one or two others may do nothing but negotiate magazine sales. Such an agency may make from one hundred fifty to three hundred book contracts a year and sell an equivalent number of short pieces to magazines. It also has an extremely large number of minor transactions such as reprints and sales in translation for small sums. The Japanese, for instance, buy rights to many American books, paying from $150 to $300 a book.

In practice, the agent is more than merely a businessman. At times he has an editorial function, although this activity is not nearly as extensive as the publisher's. For the name writer, the agent gives little, if any, editorial help. For relatively new writers, the agent may offer suggestions as to cutting of a manuscript, expansion, greater development of a character, etc. The agent also may assist in the editorial packaging and promotion of books—pressure for a good "selling jacket," more advertising, etc., as well as helping obtain agreement between author and publisher on a title that will help the sale of the book.

Not the least important function of the agent is that of father-confessor. Authors have doubts as to what to write next: fiction, non-fiction, books, or short pieces. They may be undecided between two or more ideas, or which publisher or publishing arrangement is most desirable. They can discuss these doubts with their families or friends, but neither usually is sufficiently knowledgeable to be helpful. They can talk to an editor or publisher, but it is hard to confide one's doubts to an editor with whom one expects to bargain. The agent, however, is experienced in publishing matters; he may have known the author and his work for many years; and agent and author have a mutual interest. One of the agent's functions is simply to listen, to make suggestions, and to express opinions. Thus, the author-agent relationship may result in strong personal friendship—one agent has had more than twenty books dedicated to him.

The Yellow Pages of the New York telephone book now list eighty-seven agents. Of these, some specialize in selling plays or motion pictures, and some act primarily as employment agents for actors, directors, and producers. No license is required to become an agent, and there are no formal qualifications to be met. As a result, every year individuals enter the occupation, sometimes with no office other than their apartment, and every year people fail and leave the business, almost unnoticed.

A number of the people listed as agents are not really agents, but predatory sharks. These so-called agents advertise extensively in certain writers' magazines and obtain an avalanche of manuscripts. But they do not make their living from commissions; they make their living from charging reading fees to unpublished writers. These fees may range from $10 to several hundred dollars. (In the latter case, the pseudo-agent probably would promise to have the manuscript rewritten.) In exchange for the fee, these self-styled agents then may give or pretend to give criticism, or they may offer or say they will offer the manuscript to buyers. But these so-called agents may not be competent to criticize, and most of the manuscripts they receive are so hopeless that they cannot benefit from criticism, and, of course, cannot be sold or published. Thus the author receives nothing of value for his fee. Yet these advertising sharks milk the writing trade of hundreds of thousands of dollars each year. It is a shocking racket.

Who are the legitimate agents? There is a Society of Authors' Representatives, an organization of legitimate literary agents and legitimate play brokers, all of whom make their living from commissions resulting from sales. The Society requires of its members certain standards of business practice and ethical conduct. With two or three exceptions, every literary agent and play broker who has a substantial business and a reputation for integrity and competence is a member.

How does the legitimate agent obtain his clients? He does not advertise. The professional code holds that it is as unethical for an agent to advertise as it is for a lawyer or a doctor to do so. The agent obtains clients by recommendation of his own client authors, or editors, or publishers, or perhaps by attending a writers' conference. Obtaining a client often means being in the right spot at the right time, and the agent never knows in advance what spot or time is right.

One agent on a business trip, for example, stopped in Dallas, Texas, at 9 P.M. to see an author whose first novel he admired and had just placed with a publisher. Bad weather delayed his departure until 2 A.M. the next day. By midnight, the agent had filled the author full of information about the literary business. The author then told him of a friend who was a brilliant writer, although unpublished. The agent, delighted to break the conversational monotony, went with the author to the friend's house, woke up the friend by throwing pebbles at his bedroom window, and had a long conference over highballs. The first author ultimately gave up writing but his friend became a valuable client.

A legitimate agent receives many unsolicited manuscripts from acquaintances of his clients or from people who somehow have heard of him. But he accepts few, if any, of these manuscripts, for these unpublished writers usually want an agent for the wrong reasons. They think of an agent as someone who can sell manuscripts which the author cannot sell. They are unwilling to believe what, in nine of ten cases, is the truth: that the manuscripts are poor and, hence, unsalable. Every author, published or unpublished, should realize that no agent can sell anything which the author on his own cannot sell, provided the author offers his work assiduously.

Authors often change their publishers, but once an author retains an agent, the author rarely leaves him. Joseph Wechsberg, Paul Gallico, Catherine Drinker Bowen, Thornton Wilder, Frank Slaughter, and Ogden Nash all have been with their own agents for more than twenty-five years. Yet each has had more than one publisher through the years.

Agents make mistakes. One agent received an offer of $1,000 from a motion picture company for the rights to an obscure short story published in *Argosy* magazine five or six years previously. The agent cabled the author that the offer was for $10,000. What caused the mistake the agent still does not know. He just knows that he should have had his head examined. The author cabled back, "Delighted at motion picture offer. Please accept." When the agent's idiotic clerical mistake was discovered, the author quite naturally was furious and refused to accept $1,000, and the story never was sold to pictures. Had the agent's cable given the true figure of $1,000, the author probably would have accepted. In another case, the agent for *Native Son*, by Richard Wright, failed to insert in the book contract a simple sentence that would have saved the author thousands of dollars in taxes.

Then there was the instance involving the agent for the great best seller, *Captain from Castile*, by Samuel Shellabarger. Prior to publication of the book, the agent received an offer of $40,000 from Paramount for the picture rights. The author, in need of money, told the agent to accept. Twentieth Century-Fox had also expressed interest in the book, and the agent gave Fox twenty-four hours to buy the rights for $100,-000. Fox purchased at that price, the agent was pleased with himself, and the author was in raptures. A year later, an executive of Fox, who was a friend of the agent's, told him that Fox had authorized the executive, if necessary, to pay up to $150,000. The author was out $50,000 because his agent was not a better guesser and better bargainer.

The other side of the coin is that agents can ask too much money and never sell a property. One agent, for instance, received from Metro-Goldwyn-Mayer an offer of $25,000 for rights to a novel written by a well-known literary figure. The author insisted on $35,000, which Metro refused to pay. When the novel was published, it had only a modest sale, and the picture rights never were sold.

In Hollywood the agent is omnipresent. Several agencies are enormous. The largest, William Morris & Company, has more than two hundred employees. Not merely writers, but actors, directors, and producers use agents. A person writing for motion pictures or television cannot handle his own work. Studios and producers will not read scripts offered by authors directly. Fortunately, this is not true in the print media in New York. There the agent is never obligatory.

Sometimes it is said that it is more difficult for the author of a good manuscript to find a good agent than to find a good publisher. This may well be true. An agent is busy and has a large overhead to carry. He cannot afford to sell to the minor magazines. He cannot afford to handle a writer who does not make substantial money each year. Thus most authors make their first sales themselves. Only then can they obtain the services of a legitimate agent.

CHAPTER 10 || SO YOU ARE A SUCCESS

THE author whose first novel makes a large success tends to follow a pattern. This author has awakened one fine morning to find himself famous. He is elated. The letters, the telephone calls, the requests for him to speak, to autograph copies, to do this and to do that, keep him pleasantly occupied for several months. All his friends congratulate him. A few even read his book and wonder secretly how he was able to write it. Much as he hoped for success, the rewards in acclaim and in money are far greater than he ever dreamed of. If his contracts have been properly drawn, he is carried financially for two or more years, the length of time depending upon whether his book was a book-club selection, whether it was sold to motion pictures for a large price, or perhaps just upon how many copies were sold through bookstores.

The above is all fine, but no book remains on the best-seller list forever. Royalties ultimately cease, and the author, if he is to support himself, must continue to write. No more short stories or articles for him. He writes a second novel. The publisher accepts it without waxing overenthusiastic. It is published. Compared to the first, it is an out-and-out failure. It is a tradition in the book-publishing business that second novels are poor. It is hard to explain this common occurrence. Perhaps the success of the first novel goes to the writer's head a little and as a result of cockiness and self-assurance the second book is not done with the care and the revision and the rewriting that occurred with the first book. Perhaps the idea for the first book was one which had been with the author for years and had grown upon him, while the idea for the second novel was not as carefully thought out and developed. There also may have been pure luck in the selection of the idea which proved so successful in the case of the first novel. As the author has not yet learned to evaluate his ideas and select the best, he fails to get a really good idea for his second.

Sometimes the reason for a poor second novel is the inability of the author to realize what qualities put the first one over. Often the critics or the author's friends inadvertently lead the author astray. For instance, an author writes a moving story concerning a very tall, very shy misfit of a girl from Iowa. The book moved the author as it was written, and it moved the reader. It also gave a realistic picture of growing alfalfa in Iowa, and the critics so commented. The author decides to write another novel which will give a good picture of Montana sheep raising (which he knew as a child) and also of San Francisco society (which his wife knows). The second book is a failure despite the good picture of sheep raising in Montana and of society in San Francisco. What sold the first novel, despite what the critics and the author's friends said, was the moving story, the emotional element which gripped the reader. What the second novel lacked was this emotional element.

Many professional writers fear being typed. An article writer may not want to write just about airplanes even though he is an expert in that field. Fiction writers do not want to have a reputation just as mystery writers, or just as writers of romance, or just as writers of historical novels. Many of them do not want to keep writing about their most successful characters. Sax Rohmer has hated for twenty years to write about Fu Manchu so that the author's name has almost been forgotten. Such writers fail to realize that every successful writer from Homer to modern times has to a greater or lesser extent been typed. A successful writer is known for a certain kind of story or type of writing. The reason it is so hard for article writers to build up a reputation is that their material, the subject matter they must deal with, varies so much. No one can do every kind of story equally well. Anyone who has read Irving Wallace or Conrad Richter knows that their names represent a certain kind of writing. It can be stated almost as an absolute rule that if a writer wishes to build a large reputation, if he wishes to be famous, he must be typed. The problem in the author's mind should be how well he can do the type in question, whether he has found his forte, whether he is learning to do his specialty better and better. Of course a writer should vary his material, should experiment, should try new worlds to conquer. But in trying something different, the author should do it with the idea that perhaps the new is more his forte than what he has been doing, and that hence he would like to be typed with the new. He should never change for change's sake or to avoid being typed.

Anyone who follows the careers of writers over a considerable period of years is impressed by the way they can build up a reputation by the cumulative effect of their work concentrated in one field. A couple of mysteries published in book form bring neither money nor reputation, but when twenty mysteries are published in ten years, a name emerges. Subsidiary rights become of more value and money begins to flow in. The number of books which Erle Stanley Gardner has had published partly explains his reputation and name with the reading public. In other fields than books, the situation is similar. Three or four pieces in *The New Yorker* accomplish little but twenty-five related pieces spell name and reputation. *The New Yorker* has made the reputation of Joseph Wechsberg. The adage that a rolling stone gathers no moss applies to authors. The person who writes a novel, then some short stories, then a play, then does a stint in Hollywood, and then perhaps a mystery serial is likely to find himself at the age of fifty not much further ahead than when he started. The author who can discover his forte, concentrate on it so as to be typed, is the one headed for the big time.

What is an author's forte? Many writers never even consider this problem. They want to write in a certain field for reasons they cannot explain, and they concentrate in that field. Some write Westerns, some mysteries, some only short stories, some articles, some serious novels. Some authors have a wide range; some a narrow one. Occasionally, it is late in life before an author finds his forte, discovers what he can do best; and doubtless some authors never find it at all. For twenty years Samuel Shellabarger wrote mystery novels, romances, and magazine adventure stories under various pen names. He made only a meager income. Perhaps he averaged $5,000 a year. Then he wrote *Captain from Castile,* the first of a series of best sellers in the costume field. Within a period of ten years he earned over a million dollars. Granted, he had to learn his trade as a writer and he learned it in the magazines, but still his great success did not occur until he was fifty-five years old. Perhaps it would have come much earlier had he found his forte earlier. Presumably a writer's bent is determined by his interests, his background, and perhaps by his genes. Everyone must write in the field of his experience and knowledge, but often the field in which his personal tastes lie, the field in which he personally prefers to read, is not the field in which he can write successfully. Many a successful magazine writer has *The New Yorker* as his favorite reading matter but is incapable of writing for it. One of the highest-paid writers for the *Reader's Digest* told his agent that he could get no pleasure or interest in reading the *Reader's Digest.* He said that to him the articles seemed to be written in high school English for a teen-age mentality. The late F. Scott Fitzgerald had from an early age a socialist point of view toward society. However, he was incapable of writing about the poor and afflicted. He could write delightful and brilliant stories about the rich, although intellectually his interests were connected with the poor.

Many writers as they attain success begin to ask questions to which there are no clear answers in general and perhaps no clear answers in particular cases. Should a writer write about what he knows from first-hand experience or will his imagination be less confined if he avoids direct experience? Should a writer set a story in a town he is intimately familiar with or should he invent a locality? Should his characters be composites of people he knows or should they be pure figments of his imagination? Must a writer have had a love affair in order to understand the other sex? Part of the answer to these depends on whether the writer is a romanticist or a realist, and often he does not know until he experiments in his own writing. One person is incapable of writing successfully about anything with which he is intimately familiar. Others know human nature but find their faculties are cramped by too much specific information.

Authors often wonder whether to use a pen name. If they are prolific, a pen name may be a necessity. A serious novelist usually should not publish more than one novel under his own name in a twelve-month period. If his books are published closer together, the latest one kills the sale of the previous one. Two mystery stories can be published in one year, sometimes even three. The life of such a book is short. The same situation exists for Westerns. There are authors who write six or more books a year using one or more pen names.

Some authors use a pen name for anonymity. With a real success, the secret is apt to be disclosed. Some use a pen name in the case of a sexy book to avoid reproof from their maiden aunts. Some authors will put a pen name on a manuscript they think is inferior. They want the manuscript published but do not want to hurt their names or reputations. An author may use a pen name on a book that is controversial. A prominent novelist who lives in the Deep South wrote an anti-segregation novel. He used a pen name to avoid embarrassment to his family, who had to live next to many bigoted Southern neighbors.

In the early stage of an author's career the problem of possible plagiarism is apt to bother him. How close can his story be to that of some other author's? How close can it be to a previous story of his own, already sold and published?

Forty or more years ago a story was published with the following theme and plot. On a Sunday morning a man working alone in his office in a tall office building finds himself trapped. The building is on fire, flames coming up the stairway and the elevator shaft. His position is hopeless. He telephones his girl, carries on some light badinage with her about the dress she is going to wear that coming night, and never tells her that he is about to die.

Some twelve years ago another writer sold to *Redbook* a story of a man alone on a submarine on the bottom of the sea. All the rest of the crew had been shot to the surface, but this last man could not propel himself upward. There was only half an hour's air left, but telephone communication with the surface existed. The man got connected with his girl, talked about her dress, did not let her know he was about to die.

Then a third author sold a story to the *American*. An aviator sinks an enemy vessel but has insufficient gas to get back to any ship or airfield. However, he is in radio communication with his base, and as a favor to the hero the base links him up with his girl. He talks about a dress without mentioning that he is about to die.

One further example. A while ago, *This Week* ran a story of a camper entrapped in a forest fire. He has a walkie-talkie and manages to talk to his girl about her dress, not telling her he is about to die. Only in this story a ridiculous final paragraph was added to tell that the hero escaped.

There is no evidence that any editor or magazine reader

ever noticed any similarity in the four published stories. The basic idea is identical in each story. However, the backgrounds, the characters, the plot details were different, and each author wrote differently. Had the same person written the four stories, that person might have plagiarized himself.

The problem of avoiding plagiarizing himself or plagiarizing others seldom exists for the experienced professional writer. If he builds his own story step by step, and the development of characters and action are his own, built to fit the particular story, all will be well. The fact that his plot may be that of Romeo and Juliet or that of a man carrying on light badinage with his girl and not telling her that he is about to die makes no difference.

For the article writer, the problem is somewhat different. Here his question is usually to what extent he can write two articles for two different magazines on the same subject. Of course he cannot use the same material in the two pieces, but often in getting material for one piece he runs into additional material which he hates to waste. In general, the author has to be satisfied with one article, especially if the two magazines are competitors. The answer is not so much a legal one as a common-sense one. Will the editor who publishes the second or latest one object? He will object if his readers are going to notice the similarity or feel that they are not getting something fresh and new. It is a question of degree of closeness not merely in facts but in idea and point of view.

Old age and failing powers come to all and may arrive earlier than expected, but there is no mandatory retirement age for a writer. Clarence Buddington Kelland was busily writing and selling serials to *The Saturday Evening Post* in 1958 at the age of seventy-seven. A Western writer, Vingie E. Roe, died in 1958 at the age of seventy-eight. She was two-thirds the way through a Western which seemed as good as any of her stories and which another writer did complete for her. A rental-library romance writer, Sara Ware Bassett, published a novel a year for more than fifty years, completing one in January, 1957, after her eighty-fifth birthday.

There may come a time in life when a writer has to change his type of writing. The author of gay young love stories for teenagers may find that she is getting out of touch with the young and their latest dialogue and slang and has to do something different. Sometimes a writer at any age will get into a rut from seeing the same people and doing the same things. The solution is to find new interests. If an author keeps engaging in varied activities, keeps meeting new people and seeing new places, his style and ideas will change with the changing tempo of the times. Instead of going out of style, unconsciously he will change as the style changes, and he will continue to write successfully as a part of his day and era.

One of the difficulties of the writing profession is that one's income at best is irregular and uncertain. A year's work does not necessarily produce a year's income in that twelve-month period. Often a writer forgets that if he is idle for three months he had reduced his annual income by one-fourth. After an author has finished a book it is hard to start a new book at once, and yet if he is going to make a living, that is necessary. Sir Walter Scott said that when one's dog dies one should get another dog the next day. When a book is finished, the author should start another the next day. There is a risk to the author that he may do nothing while waiting to see whether his book will be chosen by a book club or whether it will sell as a motion picture or in paperback. To avoid any such loss of time, some writers, while they are working at one book, spend a half an hour a day making notes, doing research work, and outlining their next book. They are then ready to start their new project immediately after completion of the previous one. Permanent success as a writer requires concentrated and continuous effort over a long period of time, just as in any other field of endeavor.

It is difficult for a writer to give this continuous and concentrated effort without complete solitude for several hours each working day. To a writer at work, answering a question his wife may ask, or obeying her request to let the dog out— any two-minute interruption—is a loss of ten minutes or more. One cannot immediately get back into the mood of creation on the written page. It takes time to gather one's thoughts and direct them to where one's mind was last. An author came in to see me and said:

"Paul, I am a honey-do."

I said, "What? What is the gag?"

The author continued, "Paul, I am a honey-do. My wife says Honey do this, and Honey do that, and I cannot write."

A housewife with the compulsion to write has the problem of finding consecutive time for herself. Writing is a part-time job for her, and her family may not co-operate or take her work seriously. A husband writing at home has a problem. If he were off at a job, his wife would be unable to intrude upon his working time. Some writers sleep in the daytime and work from 10 P.M. to 5 A.M. to avoid interruption. Some hire an office and keep regular office hours. Some have perceptive, well-trained, angelic wives. Many succeed despite all kinds of interruptions.

Writing may become a passion so that the urge to complete the manuscript conquers all. Winston Churchill said in a speech: "Writing a book is an adventure; to begin with it is a toy and an amusement, then it becomes a mistress, and then it becomes a master, and then it becomes a tyrant, and the last phase is that just as you are about to be reconciled to your servitude, you kill the monster and fling him about to the public."

This flinging it to the public is an emotional occurrence. Many dedicated writers find themselves lost when a long project is finished. They feel an emotion akin to bereavement and cannot feel at rest until a new venture is plotted and under way.

Many popular writers become egotistical. This is a common human failing when success is achieved. The writer is less vulnerable to this failing than the actor but more vulnerable than the successful businessman. People give a writer more direct adulation than they do a leading architect, for example. Egotism seldom promotes anyone's career, and it may have a peculiarly adverse effect on a writer. One of the characteristics of a successful writer is the ability to select the useful from the useless, the interesting from the dull; the ability to revise, discard, and add; the ability to be critical of his own writing and to take advantage of his own critical faculties to improve the manuscripts. Egotism diminishes this ability. The writer who acquires an extremely good opinion of his own powers often loses some of his critical approach, finds it difficult to imagine that what he has written is poor or subject to improvement. Hence the quality of his finished product deteriorates. There are some extremely egotistical writers who maintain a large popularity with readers. But the writer who can remain humble, who can keep his head and realize his own limited position in the current of the written word, is likely to have a greater and more permanent success.

Every professional writer is continually faced with the problem of whether to alter or revise a script at the suggestion of a critic, agent, or potential buyer. In general an author ought to consider any professional criticism, consider it with a real effort on his part to understand why the critic feels the way he does, consider it with the attitude that the critic is quite likely correct. If after such consideration the author finds that he does not agree, he should not make the change indicated. In the first place the critic may be wrong; second, even if the critic is right, the indicated change will not be effectively done if the author is unable to visualize it and honestly agree as to its desirability. By studying what a critic has to say, an author will often find that the critic is right in pointing to a weak spot. But the author may be able to cure the trouble by some different and more effective method than the critic suggested. Of course occasionally an editor will buy a script, provided an author will make an indicated change. Then the problem is simple. Does the author want the sale and check enough to make the change in question?

In general, authors are not told in advance as to the probable sale or probable success of a forthcoming book. In the case of one manuscript out of five, anything may happen. Nothing is predictable. The book may or may not be a book club selection, may or may not be sold in motion pictures, may or may not have a large bookstore sale. However, in the other four cases it is possible to predict the future with some accuracy. The bookstore and library sale can be estimated roughly. In a large number of cases one can say there is little or no chance of a book club selection. Paperback sales can often be predicted. There may be no chance of a motion picture sale. However, publishers and agents rarely tell an author the facts of life. In the first place, many authors won't believe what they are told. A diamond cutter knows diamonds, but someone dealing with books for twenty-five years is not supposed to know books. An author has his hopes, and all things pertaining to the written word are possible. Making predictions, unless they are rosy, is another way of expressing doubts, and hurts any author's feelings. After all, he has spent six months to a year struggling with a manuscript and someone who cannot write spends three hours reading the resulting effort, and then makes unpleasant statements. Who would not resent it? Publishers and agents keep quiet. Time tells the truth.

The work of all writers is uneven, is subject to a fluctuating market and to the whims of popular taste. The effect of this on a magazine author is to make rejections inevitable. Some stories are rejected by one magazine but sold to another. Many are declined by all possible markets. The author of this volume has known during the last twenty-five years only one magazine writer of standing and reputation who has sold every single piece she ever wrote, and she has had some tight squeezes. The Nobel prize winner, Pearl S. Buck, has had many rejections during the last twenty-five years and has written unsalable or second-rate manuscripts. Of course, when a successful novelist writes a poor book or a book with little popular appeal, the book is published if the author wants it published. The author's name will carry it to a considerable extent, but still the sales to the public fall off. When a well-known dramatist writes a poor play, it has a short run. Here the rejection is by the public, rather than by the editor.

All writers must have tough skins and learn to take rejections philosophically. Seldom should one believe the words in a rejection note. "In lapidary inscriptions a man is not under oath," said Samuel Johnson, and the same goes for editors writing a letter refusing a manuscript. It is hard for an editor to write an author honestly. An editor never says that a manuscript is no good, even though that may be what he privately believes. Such a statement does not help the author and just makes enemies for the editor. An editor may praise a bad manuscript but say it is not, alas, for him. Sometimes he predicts that someone else will immediately buy the manuscript. Here he is not necessarily being a hypocrite. For the author's sake, the editor hopes his opinion of the script is wrong. He knows how people disagree. He knows how hard it is to predict popular taste, and maybe someone else will buy the script. The editor is hoping that he is more selective than his rivals.

It would seem difficult for authors to save money because of the irregularity and unpredictability of their incomes. Actually they are no different from anyone else. Some save and some do not, and whether they save does not seem to have any relation to the amount they make. There are writers making from five to ten thousand dollars a year who regularly save a bit. There are those with incomes over fifty thousand a year who do not save a penny. Arthur Somers Roche, a successful magazine writer in the twenties (before the income tax amounted to much), made more than fifty thousand dollars a year for several years. He died in debt at the height of his success. Edison Marshall, a successful novelist today but also an old pro, has never earned a cent except through his pen. He has consistently saved his money, invested it conservatively, and today is a millionaire.

Writers fail, writers are half-successful, writers are successful. What are the qualities for success? There is no way of satisfactorily answering this question. However, in the opinion of the author of this volume, success as a novelist depends to a considerable measure upon a compelling urge to write and a great belief in oneself. The self-doubters never get anywhere. This belief in oneself is not a belief that what one has just written—or anything one has written—is a masterpiece, or even good. This belief in oneself is a belief that one can learn the writing trade, that with a great deal of time and effort and toil, the obstacles can be overcome. With the urge and the belief, success is not insured but it always may occur, and if the urge and the belief are strong enough, success is highly probable.

SUPPLEMENT

1. Sample form of contract for book publication
2. Sample forms used by magazines when purchasing manuscripts and rights
3. Sample freelance television film writer's contract
4. Sample contract for writing a motion picture
5. Typical translation contract
6. Sample release form for television writers
7. Organizations for writers
8. Preparing and submitting a manuscript
9. What is a literary agent? Standard practices. How to find a literary agent

Sample form of contract for book publication prepared by The Society of Authors' Representatives. Unfortunately, few publishers are willing to use this form.

AGREEMENT made this   day of   19 ,

between   , whose residence

address is   (hereinafter

called the Author); and

whose principal place of business is at

(hereinafter called the Publisher);

WITNESSETH:

In consideration of the mutual covenants herein contained, the parties agree as follows:

The Grant and the Territory.

1. The Author hereby grants and assigns to the Publisher the exclusive right to publish in the English language in book form in the United States of America, its territories and possessions, in the Philippine Islands, and in Canada, a Work now entitled "   ", (hereinafter called the Work), which title may be changed only by mutual consent in writing. All other territory (except the British Commonwealth, the Mandated Territories, and Eire) shall be an open market for the sale of English language copies of the Work published hereunder in the United States. The Author shall have the right nevertheless on sixty (60) days written notice posted to the Publisher, to withdraw the privilege of sale of cheap editions of the Work for any specified territory in such open market, in instances where the Author in

his sole discretion desires to make an exclusive contract with another for English language publication in such territory.

The Warranty.

2. The Author represents that he is the sole proprietor of the Work and that the Work to the best of his knowledge does not contain any libelous matter and does not violate the civil rights of any person or persons, does not infringe any existing copyright and has not heretofore been published in book form. The Author shall hold harmless and indemnify the Publisher from any claims, demands or recovery finally sustained by reason of any violation of copyright or other property or personal right; provided, however, that the Publisher shall with all reasonable promptness notify the Author of any claim or suit which may involve the warranties of the Author hereunder; and the Author agrees fully to cooperate in the defense thereof. The warranties contained in this Article do not extend to drawings, illustrations, or other material not furnished by the Author.

The Manuscript.

3. The Author agrees to deliver to the Publisher not later than   19   , a complete typewritten script of the work. If the script shall not have been delivered within three (3) months after said date the Publisher may, at its option, terminate this agreement by notice in writing posted or delivered to the Author and may recover from the Author all monies which it may have advanced to the Author upon the Work.

Publication of the Work.

4. The Publisher agrees to publish the Work at its own expense at a catalogue retail price of not less than
                              Dollars ($) per copy on or before   months after the delivery of the completed Work. In the event of delay from causes beyond the control of the Publisher, the publication date may be postponed accordingly, but not to exceed   months. In case of first serialization, book publication shall be delayed until serial publication is completed.

The Copyright.

5. The Publisher, upon first publication of the Work, agrees duly to copyright it in the United States of America and Canada in the name of the Author, and to imprint the copyright notice required by law in each copy of the work. The Author agrees to furnish the Publisher promptly with any authorization or other document necessary to carry out the provisions hereof.

The Author shall, upon the termination of the first term, make timely application for renewal of copyright under then existing United States Copyright Law and, provided this contract shall then be in force and effect, the Author agrees to assign to the Publisher, for the renewal term of the copyright, the rights herein granted to the Publisher.

Printer's Proofs.

6. The Publisher shall furnish the Author with galley proof and, on request, page proof of the Work which, except for changes in styling required by the Publisher, shall conform to the completed manuscript as submitted by the Author, without changes in, additions to, or eliminations from such manuscript. The Author agrees to return such proof to the Publisher with his corrections within thirty (30) days of the receipt thereof by him. The cost of alterations in the galley proof or page proof required by the Author, other than corrections of printer's errors, in excess of fifteen (15%) per cent of the original cost of composition, shall be charged against the earnings of the Author under this agreement or shall, at the option of the Publisher, be paid by the Author in cash; provided, however, that in such case, the Publisher shall upon request promptly furnish to the Author an itemized statement of such additional expenses, and shall make available at the Publisher's office the corrected proof for inspection by the Author or his representatives.

Advances, Royalties and Share of Proceeds; Examination of Accounts.

7. The Publisher shall pay to the Author or his duly authorized representatives, the following advances and royalties:

(a) An advance of $ against the Author's
earnings under this agreement payable

(b) A royalty upon the regular edition sold in the United
States of
> per cent (%) of the retail price thereof
> on the first copies sold
> per cent (%) on the next   copies sold
> per cent (%) on all copies sold
> in excess of

(c) A royalty of fifteen per cent (15%) of the amount of
the Publisher's charges for bound copies of the original
edition of the Work and eighteen per cent (18%) for
unbound sheets, sold for export, and to reading circles,
to recognized book clubs, and to organizations outside
the regular book selling channels, provided that such
sales are made at a discount of sixty per cent (60%)
or more from the retail price. Such royalties shall be
payable without deduction for discounts or bad debts.

(d) Two-thirds (2/3) of any license fee charged a Canadian
publisher for the right to publish the Work on a royalty
basis or for an outright sum, in Canada.

(e)   per cent (%) of the retail price of each copy sold of any cheap edition issued
by the Publisher at a retail price not more than two-
thirds (2/3) of the original retail price.

(f)   per cent (%) of any license fee charged
for the right granted another Publisher to issue and dis-
tribute a cheap edition of the Work.

(g)   per cent (%) of the gross amount paid
by a book club, whether as plate rental or royalty or
otherwise, for the right to publish the Work in whole or
in part for distribution to its members.

(h) Ten per cent (10%) of the amount of the Publisher's charges for copies of overstock which the Publisher deems expedient to sell at a discount of seventy per cent (70%) or more; provided that if such sale is made at or below cost of manufacture, no royalty shall be paid. If the Publisher determines to remainder its entire stock, it shall give the Author reasonable notice in advance thereof. No sale of overstock may take place before the expiration of one (1) year from the first publication of the Work in book form.

(i) Three quarters (3/4) of the stipulated royalty on all copies sold from a reprinting of   copies or less made after two (2) years from the date of the first publication hereunder and provided that the regular sales in the six-month period preceding such reprinting did not exceed   (   ) copies; the reduction of royalties provided for in this sub-division is to enable the publisher to keep the Work in print and in circulation as long as possible.

No royalties shall be payable on free copies furnished to the Author or on copies for review, sample, or other similar purposes, or on copies destroyed.

No cheap edition in any category may be published earlier than one (1) year from the date of the original publication.

The Author or his duly authorized representatives shall have the right upon written request to examine the books of account of the Publisher insofar as they relate to the Work; such examination shall be at the cost of the Author unless errors of accounting amounting to five (5%) per cent or more of the total sum paid to the Author shall be found to his disadvantage, in which the cost shall be borne by the Publisher.

Overpayment.

8. In all instances in which the Author shall have received an overpayment of monies under the terms hereof, the Publisher may deduct such overpayment from any further sums payable to the Author either in respect to the Work or under other contracts between the Author and Publisher for any other

books; provided, however, that the term "overpayment" shall not in any event apply to unearned advances.

Permission to Reprint.

9. The Publisher may permit others to reprint selections from the Work in text books, or anthologies designed for text book use, and payments made for such permission shall be equally divided between the Author and Publisher. The Publisher may grant permission to publish extracts of the Work containing not more than five hundred (500) words, without compensation therefor.

Contracts with Others.

10. The Publisher agrees promptly to advise the Author of the terms of any contracts entered into for any grant or license permitted under this agreement whenever the Author's share of the proceeds or royalty is One Hundred ($100.) Dollars or more. Such contracts shall be made available by the Publisher to the Author or his representative at the office of the Publisher, and a copy thereof will be furnished the Author upon his written request.

Free Copies.

11. The Publisher agrees to present to the Author ten (10) free copies of the regular edition of the Work and three (3) copies of any cheap edition published, and the Author shall be permitted to purchase further copies for his personal use at a discount of forty (40%) per cent from the retail price.

Statements and Payments.

12. The Publisher agrees to render semi-annual statements in duplicate on   and
in each year following the publication hereof, showing an account of sales and all other payments due hereunder to
                              and
preceding said respective accounting dates. Payments then due shall accompany such statements.

Termination and Reversion of Rights.

13. (a) In the event that the Work shall at any time be out of print, the Author or his representative may give notice

thereof to the Publisher, and in such event the Publisher shall declare within thirty (30) days in writing whether or not he intends to bring out a new edition of the Work; if he shall declare his intention to bring out such new edition, then such edition shall be published not later than six (6) months from the giving of such notice. If the Publisher shall not within thirty (30) days declare in writing that he does so intend, and shall not within six (6) months bring out a new printing of the Work, then all rights granted hereunder shall terminate and revert to the Author at the end of such thirty (30) days, or six (6) month period, as the case may be.

If the Work be out of print and Publisher gives the Author three (3) months notice in writing of its intention to discontinue publication, then this agreement shall terminate at the expiration of said three (3) month period.

The Work shall not be considered to be out of print if it is on sale in a cheap edition or in any other edition, in the United States, or if there shall be in existence a contract for cheap edition publication which provides for publication within (   ) months after the Work is out of print in the regular edition.

(b) If the Publisher shall, during the existence of this agreement, default in the delivery of semi-annual statements or in the making of payments as herein provided and shall neglect or refuse to deliver such statements or make such payments, or any of them, within thirty (30) days after written notice of such default, this agreement shall terminate at the expiration of such thirty (30) days without prejudice to the Author's claim for any monies which may have accrued under this agreement or to any other rights and remedies to which the Author may be entitled.

(c) If the Publisher shall fail to publish the Work within the period in Paragraph 4 provided, or otherwise fail to comply with or fulfill the terms and conditions hereof, or in the event of bankruptcy, etc., as in Paragraph 14 hereof provided, this agreement shall terminate and the rights herein granted to Publisher shall revert to the Author. In such event all payments theretofore made to the Author shall belong to the Author without prejudice to any other remedies which the Author may have.

(d) Upon the termination of this agreement for any cause under this Article or Article 14 hereof, all rights granted to the Publisher shall revert to the Author for his use at any time and the Publisher shall return to the Author all property originally furnished by the Author; the Author shall have the right in such instance to purchase the plates from the Publisher at their metal value, and any or all of the remaining sheets or copies at a price not to exceed fifty (50%) per cent of the manufacturing cost, exclusive of overhead. If the Author shall not have acquired such plates, sheets or copies within ( ) days of the effective date of such termination, the Publisher shall have the right to sell such remaining copies at cost or less, without payment to the Author of royalties on such sales. If the Publisher shall desire to melt such plates, he shall give the Author ( ) days notice in writing thereof and an opportunity to acquire such plates as above provided. No such sale by the Publisher shall transfer the right of publication and sale of the Work to any purchaser of the remaining copies or sheets. The Publisher's privilege to sell the remaining copies shall expire six (6) months after the effective termination date and thereupon all remaining copies shall be destroyed. In the event that the parties shall have agreed to the taking of the copyright in the name of the Publisher, then the Publisher shall, upon such termination, furnish the Author an assignment of such copyright to him in due form for recording.

Bankruptcy and Insolvency.

14. If a petition in bankruptcy shall be filed by or against the Publisher, or if it shall be adjudged insolvent by any court, or if a Trustee or a Receiver of any property of the Publisher shall be appointed in any suit or proceeding by or against the Publisher, or if the Publisher shall make an assignment for the benefit of creditors or shall take the benefit of any bankruptcy or insolvency Act, or if the Publisher shall liquidate its business for any cause whatsoever, this agreement shall terminate automatically without notice, and such termination

shall be effective as of date of the filing of such petition, adjudication, appointment, assignment or declaration or commencement of reorganization or liquidation proceedings, and all rights granted hereunder shall thereupon revert to the Author. As a condition of the making of this agreement the Author hereby acquires the right, upon such termination, to purchase at his option the plates, remaining copies and sheets as provided in Article 13 hereof. In the event that the Author's option to purchase such properties is not exercised within thirty (30) days after the Author has had notice of the happening of the event herein referred to, the Publisher, Trustee, Receiver, Assignee or other such official, may melt the plates and sell the copies or sheets remaining on hand subject only to payment to the Author of the royalties herein provided. In the event the Author desires to purchase the books and sheets aforesaid, and the Trustee, Receiver or other said named official deems the price fixed at fifty (50%) per cent of the manufacturing cost or the metal value to be below the fair market value thereof, then such value shall be determined by arbitration conducted pursuant to commercial arbitration rules of the American Arbitration Association then applicable.

Reserved Rights.

15. All rights in the Work now existing, or which may hereafter come into existence, not specifically herein granted, are reserved to the Author for his use at any time. Reserved publication rights include, but are not limited to, the right to publish or cause to be published in any form, excerpts, summaries and novelizations of dramatizations and motion pictures of the Work, thereof, not to exceed seventy-five hundred (7500) words in length, to be used for advertising and exploitation of motion pictures and televised motion pictures or dramatizations based upon the Work.

Assignment.

16. No assignment of this contract, voluntary or by operation of law, shall be binding upon either of the parties without the written consent of the other; provided, however, that the Author may assign or transfer any monies due or to become due under this agreement.

Arbitration.

17. Any controversy or claim arising out of this agreement or the breach thereof shall be settled by arbitration in accordance with the rules then obtaining of the American Arbitration Association, and judgment upon the award may be entered in the highest court of the forum, State or Federal, having jurisdiction. Such arbitration shall be held in the City of New York unless otherwise agreed by the parties. The Author may at his option, in case of failure to pay royalties, refuse to arbitrate, and pursue his legal remedies.

Notices.

18. Any written notice required under any of the provisions of this agreement shall be deemed to have been properly served by delivery in person or by mailing the same to the parties hereto at the addresses set forth above, except as the addresses may be changed by notice in writing; provided, however, that notices of termination shall be sent by registered mail.

Waiver.

19. A waiver of any breach of this agreement or of any of the terms or conditions by either party thereto, shall not be deemed a waiver of any repetition of such breach or in any wise affect any other terms or conditions hereof; no waiver shall be valid or binding unless it shall be in writing, and signed by the parties.

Special Arrangements.

20.

Agency.

21. The Author hereby authorizes his agent to collect and receive all sums of money payable to him under the terms of this agreement and the receipt of such agent shall be a good and valid discharge in respect thereof. The said agent is hereby fully authorized and empowered to act on be-

half of the Author in all matters in any way arising out of this agreement.

Interpretation.

22. Regardless of the place of its physical execution, this contract shall be interpreted under the laws of the State of New York and of the United States of America.

IN WITNESS WHEREOF the parties hereto have duly executed this agreement the day and year first above written.

In the   (seal)   _____
Presence of: Publisher

_____   By_____
In the presence of: (   )

_____   _____
                                                                 Author

Sample form used by McCall Corporation accompanying payment for manuscript, showing rights purchased.

McCALL CORPORATION
230 PARK AVENUE, NEW YORK, N.Y. 10017 • (212) 983-3200

McCALL'S Magazine

TO: Contract No.
                                       Requisition No.
                                       Order No.
                                       Date

This will confirm our purchase of rights in and to the literary material entitled .... (the "material") by .... (the "author") submitted by .... (the "agent"), as follows:

1. In consideration of the sum of $............. (in payment of which we herewith enclose our check), the author grants to McCall Corporation, its licensees and assigns, all rights in and to the material and all rights of copyright therein, including, but without limitation, the exclusive North American serial rights therein, namely, the right to publish the same in original, condensed or other form (and to authorize and issue reprints and digests) in magazines and newspapers in the United States and Canada, and the right of any incidental distribution in other foreign countries. The rights herein granted include the right: to edit, revise, abridge, condense and translate the material; to publish the same in one or more installments; to change the title thereof; to use the author's name, biography and likeness in connection with the publication, advertising and promotion of said material; and to make such other promotional use of the material as McCall Corporation may determine.

2. McCall Corporation agrees to reconvey to the author, 90 days after the first completed publication of said material, all

rights in and to the copyright secured on said material, except the exclusive North American serial rights therein hereinabove defined.

3. The author warrants that he is the author and sole owner of the material, that it is original and has never been published in any form, that it contains no matter unlawful in content or violative of the rights of any third party, that the rights granted hereunder are free and clear, and that he has full power to grant such rights.

4. The author's agent represents that he has full authority from the author to dispose of the author's rights in said material in accordance with the foregoing terms and conditions and to make in behalf of the author the warranties set out in paragraph 3 above.

Acceptance of the enclosed check will constitute your agreement to and acceptance of the foregoing terms and conditions.

McCALL CORPORATION

By . . . .
Authorized Signature

Form B - Contribution to a Periodical
Grant of All Rights
With Agreement to Reconvey

Sample form used by Fawcett Publications, Inc., accompanying payment for manuscript, showing rights purchased.

FAWCETT PUBLICATIONS, INC.

Author's Agreement

$_____

Received from Fawcett Publications, Inc., the above mentioned sum as payment in full for the manuscript or work entitled_____by_____
_____and all literary property and other rights therein, including complete publication rights and the right to copyright same in the name of Fawcett Publications, Inc. and to make editorial changes therein deemed necessary.

The undersigned warrants the originality, authorship and ownership of said work; and grants to Fawcett Publications, Inc. the right to publish or authorize the publication of the author's name and picture in connection with the publication of said work, or advertise same, including the right to publicize said work in such a way as Fawcett Publications may desire in connection with the Fawcett magazine in which said work is published. Sixty days after publication by Fawcett Publications, Inc. it will reassign to the author, upon written request, all rights in said work, except the right to publish same in original, digest or other form in magazines or periodicals published in the United States of America or its possessions. After reassignment of such rights, the author shall at all times cause the rights in said work reserved by Fawcett Publications, Inc. to be protected by proper copyright notice.

Dated: , 19 _____

Sample freelance television film writer's contract.

AGREEMENT DATED: _____ , between

PRODUCER:

WRITER: _____

Writer's Notice Address: _____

_____

_____

Attention: _____

1. *SERIES:* _____ PROD. NO. _____

    EPISODE TITLE: _____ LENGTH _____

2. *FORM OF WORK:* _____

3. *COMPENSATION:*

    (a) *Basic:*

        (i) On Delivery of Revised Story: $

        (ii) On Exercise of Teleplay Option,
               If Any: $

        (iii) On Delivery of First-Draft
                Teleplay/Rewrite/Polish: $

        (iv) On Delivery of Final-Draft
                Teleplay/Rewrite/Polish: $

        (v) Other: $_____

    Aggregate Basic Compensation: $_____

(b) *Residuals:* Should Writer become entitled to compensation for television re-runs or foreign telecasts, or to theatrical release compensation with respect to the work pursuant to the Minimum Basic Agreement, Producer agrees to pay, and Writer agrees to accept therefor, the minimum additional compensation provided in the Minimum Basic Agreement subject to and in accordance with the applicable provisions of the Minimum Basic Agreement, including but not limited to its prorating provisions should another writer or writers be entitled to share therein.

4. *DELIVERY AND READING TIME:*

(a) *Commencement Date for Services:* _____

(b) *Delivery of First-Draft Story:* Writer shall deliver the First-Draft Story to Producer not later than:

> ½-hour: 7 days ⎫
> 1-hour: 10 days ⎬ after commencement of services pursuant to (a) above.
> 1½-hour: 14 days ⎭

(c) *Reading Time of First-Draft Story:* Producer shall request any desired revisions in the First-Draft Story not later than 7 days after Writer's actual delivery thereof to Producer.

(d) *Delivery of Revised Story:* Writer shall deliver the Revised Story, incorporating the revisions requested by Producer pursuant to (c) above, not later than:

> ½-hour: 7 days ⎫
> 1-hour: 10 days ⎬ after Producer's request pursuant to (c) above.
> 1½-hour: 14 days ⎭

(e) *Reading Time of Revised Story:* Producer shall exercise, if at all, its option, if any, to require Writer to write the teleplay based on the Revised Story not later than 14 days after Writer's actual delivery of the Revised Story to Producer; provided that Producer shall have the right, but not the obligation, to request a second revision of the Story within such 14-day period on either of the following bases:

(i) That such second revision shall be made in the execution of the First-Draft Teleplay; or

(ii) That such second revision shall be made in the Revised Story, in which event Producer shall be obligated to pay Writer additional basic compensation for the Story as revised by such second revision equal to 50% of the amount provided in Paragraph 3,(a),(i), and Producer's option, if any, to require Writer to write the teleplay based upon the Story as so revised shall be extended for a period of 7 days following the delivery by Writer to Producer of the Revised Story incorporating such second revision. Producer may also, in such event, require a third revision of the Story to be incorporated in the First-Draft Teleplay.

(f) *Delivery of First-Draft Teleplay:* Writer shall deliver the First-Draft Teleplay, incorporating all revisions Producer has been entitled to request, to Producer not later than:

½-hour: 14 days ⎱ after date of Producer's last
1-hour: 21 days ⎰ request for revisions pursuant
1½-hour: 28 days ⎱ to (c), or (e), as the case may be.

(g) *Reading Time of First-Draft Teleplay:* Producer shall request any desired revisions in the First-Draft Teleplay not later than:

½-hour: 7 days ⎱ after Writer's actual
1-hour or longer: 14 days ⎰ delivery thereof to Producer.

(h) *Delivery of Revised First-Draft Teleplay:* Writer shall deliver the Revised First-Draft Teleplay, incorporating Producer's requested revisions pursuant to (g) above, to Producer not later than 7 days after Producer's request pursuant to (g) above.

(i) *Reading Time of Revised First-Draft Teleplay:* Producer shall request any desired revisions in the Revised First-Draft Teleplay not later than 7 days after Writer's actual delivery thereof to Producer.

(j) *Delivery of Final-Draft Teleplay:* Writer shall deliver the Final-Draft Teleplay, incorporating Producer's requested revisions above, to Producer not later than 7 days after Producer's request pursuant to (i) above.

5. *ENGAGEMENT:*

Producer hereby employs Writer to write the literary material described in Article 2 hereof, hereinafter for convenience referred to as the "work". Writer accepts such employment and agrees to render his services hereunder and to devote his best talents, efforts and abilities thereto in accordance with the instructions and directions of Producer, all on the terms and conditions contained in this Agreement.

Writer acknowledges and agrees that the work shall be based upon literary or dramatic material rights in which are owned by Producer under conditions whereby Article XX (Separation of Rights) of the Minimum Basic Agreement shall not apply to the work; and that due delivery of the several stages of the work within the times provided above is of the essence of this Agreement, and Writer's failure to meet said delivery schedule for any reason shall be a material and substantial breach of this Agreement.

The parties acknowledge that this Agreement is subject to all of the applicable provisions of the Producer-Writers Guild of America Minimum Basic Film Television Agreement of 1966 (herein referred to as the "Minimum Basic Agreement").

6. *WARRANTIES:*

Subject to the limitations provided for in the Minimum Basic Agreement, Writer hereby warrants and agrees that all material written by him hereunder shall be wholly original with him and shall not be copied in whole or in part from any other work except that submitted to Writer by Producer. Subject as aforesaid, Writer further warrants and agrees that neither the said material nor any part thereof will violate the right of privacy of nor libel any person, firm or corporation nor will said material or any part thereof infringe any copyright, literary, dramatic, photoplay or common law rights of any person, firm or corporation. Writer further agrees subject as aforesaid, that he will hold Producer and its successors, licensees and assigns harmless against all liability, loss, damage or expense, including reasonable counsel fees, which they or any of them may suffer or incur by reason of the breach of any of the warranties made herein.

7. *GRANT OF RIGHTS:*

Subject to the provisions of the Minimum Basic Agreement, Writer agrees that all the material written by him hereunder shall be and become the property of Producer as the employer of Writer for hire. Producer shall be deemed to be the author-at-law thereof, and (subject to the provisions of the Minimum Basic Agreement) shall own all rights therein. Producer shall have the right to change, alter, revise, add to or subtract from the work in Producer's sole discretion, and the right to combine the work with material furnished or created by others.

Producer shall have no obligation to produce any motion picture based upon or using the work or to use the work in any other manner whatsoever. Subject to the provisions of the Minimum Basic Agreement, no rights in the work shall revert to the Writer under any circumstances.

Concurrently with the execution of this Agreement, Writer has executed and delivered to Producer a Certificate of Authorship to be used to identify the completed work. Writer hereby authorizes Producer, as Writer's attorney-in-fact for such purpose, to insert in said Certificate, as the various steps of the work are delivered, descriptions of said work, and to insert a date in such Certificate, which date shall be the business day on which the completed work is delivered to Producer. In addition Writer will, at the request of Producer, execute and deliver to Producer, in connection with all such material, such assignments or other instruments as Producer may from time to time deem necessary or desirable to evidence, establish, maintain, protect, enforce or defend its right, title or interest in or to such material. Writer hereby appoints Producer the true and lawful attorney-in-fact of Writer, irrevocably, to execute, acknowledge and deliver any such instruments or documents which Writer shall fail or refuse to execute, acknowledge or deliver.

Writer grants to Producer the perpetual non-exclusive right to use, and to license others to use, his name, likeness and biography in connection with his employment hereunder, or any results and proceeds thereof, and in advertising or exploiting any one or more of the television pictures based on the work, or a series in which any one or more of said pictures may be contained, or the products and/or services of any sponsor or sponsors of such television pictures, or series, this grant, however, not to include any product endorsement by Writer without the specific written consent of Writer in each instance.

8. *PUBLIC OPINION:*
   Writer agrees to conduct himself with due regard to public conventions and morals. Writer also agrees not to do or commit any act or thing that will degrade him or subject him to public hatred, contempt, scorn, ridicule or disrepute, or shock or offend the community or violate public morals or decency, or prejudice his standing in the community or the Producer or the motion picture, theatrical, television, radio, or entertainment industry in general, or that will tend to do any of the foregoing.

9. *GUILD MEMBERSHIP:*
   To the extent that it may be lawful for the Producer to require the Writer so to do, Writer agrees to become and/or remain a member of Writers Guild of America, West, Inc., in good standing as required by the provisions of the Minimum Basic Agreement. As a condition to Writer's employment hereunder, Writer agrees that Producer may, if it so elects, and if legally permissible, pay any dues or assessments which may be or become payable by Writer to such Union, or which may be required to establish or maintain Writer's membership in good standing in such Union, and that Producer may deduct the amount of such payment from any compensation then or thereafter due to Writer from Producer. Writer hereby expressly authorizes Producer to make any and all such deductions and payments and agrees that the payment thereof shall, to the extent of such payment, discharge Producer's obligation with respect to the payment of compensation then or thereafter due to Writer from Producer. Producer shall be entitled to rely upon any information furnished by such Union with respect to any dues or assessments which may be or become payable by Writer to such Union, or which may be required to estab-

lish or maintain Writer's membership in good standing in such Union, and Producer shall not be liable to Writer for any payment or overpayment to such Union based upon such information nor shall Producer be under any obligation to Writer to take any steps whatsoever to reclaim or recover such payment or overpayment from such Union. If Writer fails or refuses to become or remain a member of said Union in good standing, as required in the first sentence of this Article, Producer shall have the right at any time thereafter to terminate this Agreement with Writer.

10. *CREDIT:*
The provisions of Article XI of the Minimum Basic Agreement (as amended from time to time) shall govern the matter of such credit, if any, as is to be accorded to Writer hereunder.

11. *NOTICES:*
Except as provided in Article XXIX of the Minimum Basic Agreement, all notices which Producer is required or may desire to serve upon Writer under or in connection with this Agreement may be served by addressing the same to Writer at such address as he may designate from time to time in writing, or if Writer fails to so designate an address, or having so designated an address, cancels such address and fails to so designate a new address, then by addressing the same to Writer at any place where Producer has a studio or an office, and in any case, by depositing the same so addressed, postage prepaid, in the United States mail, or by sending the same so addressed by telegraph or cable, or at its option, Producer may deliver the same to Writer personally either in writing, or unless otherwise specified herein, orally. If Producer elects to mail such notice or to send the same by telegraph or cable, then the date of the mailing thereof (whether the same be sent by registered mail, with or without return receipt requested, certified mail, airmail and/or ordinary mail) or the date of delivery thereof to the telegraph or cable office, as the case may be, shall be the date of the service of such notice.

12. *PROHIBITED MATERIAL:*
Writer acknowledges that he is familiar with the provisions of sections 317 and 508, Communications Act Amend-

ments, 1960; and agrees and warrants that he shall not insert or include in the work any literary or dramatic material or program material the nature of which would require an announcement or disclosure in order to comply with the provisions of said section 317 or 508, unless Producer has given to Writer its prior written consent specifically to such inclusion or insertion and provision has been made for the appropriate announcement or disclosure, or both, as the case may be.

13. *MORE THAN ONE WRITER:*

In the event that more than one writer is named as party hereto, the word "Writer" whenever and wherever used herein shall be deemed to mean "Writers" and all other references herein to "Writer" shall be deemed to be references to such "Writers". Such Writers shall be treated as a unit for purposes of compensation hereunder, and the compensation payable hereunder shall be payable to them in equal shares unless they otherwise direct Producer in writing signed by all such Writers or unless otherwise required by the Minimum Basic Agreement.

14. *CONTINGENCIES:*

Producer shall have the right to terminate Writer's employment hereunder in the event that, while rendering services hereunder or while obligated to render services hereunder or prior thereto,   (a) Writer should be incapacitated or prevented from performing his obligations hereunder for a period or aggregate of periods in excess of one (1) week because of Writer's illness or other incapacity or for any cause rendering such nonperformance excusable at law; or   (b) the preparation or production of photoplays by Producer or the conduct of Producer's business generally is materially hampered, interrupted or interfered with by any matter or thing beyond Producer's control for a period or aggregate of periods in excess of four (4) weeks; or   (c) Writer should fail, refuse or neglect to faithfully perform any of Writer's obligations or covenants hereunder, or to render any of Writer's required services hereunder. In the event Writer's employment hereunder is terminated pursuant to any of the provisions of this Article, Producer shall upon such termination be released from all further obligations and liability to Writer whatsoever other than to pay Writer such compensation, if any, as shall be due Writer hereunder at the time of such termination and is unpaid; residuals, if any, which may become due by reason of Writer's participation in credit with respect to the work; and credit required to be accorded to Writer pursuant to the Minimum Basic Agreement. Producer shall retain and own all rights of every kind (subject to the provisions of the Minimum Basic Agreement) in and to all material theretofore written or prepared by Writer hereunder, and in and to all other results and proceeds of any and all services theretofore rendered by Writer hereunder.

15. *MISCELLANEOUS:*

(a) No waiver by either of the parties hereto of any failure by the other party to keep or perform any covenant or condition of this Agreement shall be deemed to be a waiver of any preceding or succeeding breach of the same or any other covenant or condition.

(b) Neither the expiration of this Agreement nor any other termination hereof shall affect Producer's rights under Article 7 hereof or release Writer from any warranty or undertaking on the part of Writer hereunder, except his obligation to perform further services.

(c) This Agreement relates solely to Writer's employment for writing the material referred to herein and shall not, except as otherwise specifically stated herein, affect any agreement between Producer and Writer relating to other matters. This Agreement constitutes the entire understanding between Writer and Producer concerning the subject matter hereof and shall not be modified, changed, renewed, extended or discharged except as specifically provided herein, or by an agreement in writing signed by the party against whom enforcement of such change, modification, renewal, extension or discharge is sought.

(d) Producer may sublicense any and all rights herein, or any portion thereof, or the material furnished hereunder, and may assign this Agreement, or any and all of such rights as Producer may elect.

(e) Any right or obligation of either Writer or Producer hereunder which is not specifically covered and controlled by the express terms of this Agreement shall be governed and controlled by the terms and provisions of the Minimum Basic Agreement, subject, of course, to the provisions of Article 5 hereof. Writer shall be entitled to the minimum benefits derived thereunder and Producer shall be entitled to the maximum benefits derived thereunder.

IN WITNESS WHEREOF, the parties hereto have duly executed this Agreement on the day and year first above written.

_____
"Producer"

_____
"Writer"

_____
"Writer"

Sample contract for writing a motion picture.

January 16, 1968

Dear Mr. —————— :

This will confirm your employment agreement with the under-signed (herein referred to as "we", "us" or their equivalent) as follows:

1. We hereby employ you to write, on a flat deal basis, for and in connection with a feature length motion picture photo-play now entitled
hereinafter referred to as the "Photoplay", a complete and finished screenplay. Nothing herein contained shall preclude you from engaging in other minor and incidental activities simultaneously with you writing the screenplay which do not hamper or interfere with your writing the screenplay includ-ing but not limited to your employment by us as associate producer.

The literary material which you shall write for and in con-nection with the Photoplay shall be based upon such material and/or ideas selected by us and assigned to you, including your novel entitled

The term "Photoplay" or its equivalent as used herein shall be deemed to include but not be limited to a motion picture production photographed in black and white or in color, pro-duced and/or exhibited with and/or accompanied by sound and voice recording, reproducing and/or transmitting devices, radio devices, television devices and all developments and im-provements of such devices and all other devices or improve-ments which are now or hereafter may be used in connection with the production, exhibition and/or transmission of any present or future kind of motion picture productions and which motion picture production may be distributed theatrically or non-theatrically, in any size, type or gauge film and in con-junction with the advertising of any product, commodity or service.

2. You hereby accept such employment upon all of the terms and conditions herein contained, and agree to keep and perform all of the obligations and agreements assumed and entered into by you hereunder. The term of your employment shall commence or be deemed to have commenced on the date to be designated by us by not less than three (3) weeks' written notice to you, and the term of your employment shall continue thereafter until you have fully and completely written all of the literary material and rendered all other services required of you hereunder, or unless sooner terminated in accordance with the provisions of this agreement.

You agree to complete and deliver to us the literary material required of you hereunder on or before the expiration of the following stipulated periods of time:

(a) First draft screenplay: twelve (12) weeks from and after the commencement date hereof as specified herein:

(b) First set of changes, revisions, deletions and/or additions: six (6) weeks from and after delivery to us of the completed first draft screenplay, it being understood that we shall have the right to review and discuss with you the nature of such changes, revisions, deletions and/or additions during the first two (2) weeks of said six (6) week period:

(c) Final draft screenplay, including second set of changes, revisions, deletions and/or additions: six (6) weeks from and after delivery to us of the completed first set of changes, revisions, deletions, and/or additions: provided, that we shall have the right to review and discuss with you the nature of such changes, revisions, deletions and/or additions during the first two (2) weeks of said six (6) week period.

3. On condition that you shall fully and completely keep and perform all of your obligations and agreements hereunder, and as full consideration for any and all services rendered by you for us, and for all rights granted and/or agreed to be granted by you to us, we agree to pay you, and you agree to

accept, the total sum of Fifty Thousand Dollars ($50,000.00) which sum shall be payable as follows:

(a) $2,500.00 upon commencement of your services hereunder:

(b) $5,000.00 upon completion and delivery by you to us of the first sixty (60) pages of the screenplay:

(c) $5,000.00 upon delivery to us of the completed first draft screenplay:

(d) $2,500.00 upon delivery to us of the completed first set of changes, revisions, deletions and/or additions:

(e) $2,500.00 upon delivery to us of the completed second set of changes, revisions, deletions and/or additions:

(f) $10,000.00 upon commencement of principal photography of the Photoplay, but not later than the exercise by us of our option to acquire motion picture and other rights in and to the novel
if we exercise our option therefore under our option agreement with you: it being agreed that the sum of $10,000.00 under this subparagraph (f) and $22,500.00 under the following Subparagraph (g) shall not become payable if we fail to exercise said option on or before its expiration.

(g) $22,500.00 in two (2) equal installments each of $11,250.00 on January 10 of the first and second years following the calendar year in which we exercise the aforementioned option.

With regard to Subparagraphs (a) through (e) herein, no compensation shall be due or payable to you for any period or periods during which you shall fail, refuse or neglect, or shall be unable for any reason to render your services as required or desired by us under the terms of this agreement. It is agreed that you shall not be entitled to any additional compensation in the event that you shall be required to render your services hereunder for a period in excess of the stipulated periods of time designated in Paragraph 2 hereof in order to complete all of the literary material required of you hereunder.

No additional compensation shall accrue or be payable to you by reason of the fact that any of your services are rendered at night, on Sundays, or holidays, or after the expiration of any particular number of hours of service in any period. If we fail to designate a commencement date for your services under Paragraph 2 hereof prior to the expiration of four (4) months after the date hereof, we shall nonetheless pay you the compensation set forth hereinabove as if such commencement date were four (4) months after the date hereof, and in such event you shall render your services hereunder on such later commencement date, if any, as we may designate without any additional compensation therefor.

4. You represent that you are free to enter into this agreement and that you have not made and will not hereafter make any commitment or agreement which could or might interfere with the full and complete rendition of your services hereunder. You agree that throughout the term hereof you will render your services solely and exclusively for us and as, when and wherever we may require. Without limiting the generality of the foregoing, you shall render your services at such studio and on such locations as we may designate. You agree to render your services in a diligent and conscientious manner and to the best of your ability, to show us and/or deliver to us whenever requested all material theretofore written by you hereunder, and to comply promptly and faithfully with all reasonable instructions, directions, requests, rules and regulations (including those related to matters of artistic taste and judgment) made or issued by us. You agree to render your services under the supervision, direction and control of and/or in collaboration with such person or persons as we may from time to time designate. You agree to render all services usually and customarily rendered by and required of writers employed to write literary material in the motion picture industry. You agree that you will not divulge or make known to any person, firm or corporation any of the terms or subject matter of this agreement, or any matters of a confidential nature pertaining to our business without our express written consent first had and obtained. During the term hereof, you shall not render services of any kind whatever for any person, firm or corporation other than ourselves, or for or on your own behalf, without our express written consent first had and obtained.

5. You warrant and agree that all material of whatever kind, written, prepared, composed and/or submitted by you hereunder for or to us, shall be wholly original with you and shall not be copied in whole or part from any other work and shall not infringe upon or violate the right of privacy of, or constitute a libel against, or violate any copyright, common law right, or any other right of any person, firm or corporation. The foregoing warranties shall not apply to any material taken directly by you from any material assigned by us to you for adaptation or revision, but shall apply to all material, incidents, characterizations and treatment which you may add to or interpolate in such assigned material. You agree to indemnify and hold us harmless from and against any loss, liability, judgment, cost or expense of any kind and character suffered or incurred by us by reason of any adjudicated breach by you of any of the foregoing warranties. The provisions of this Paragraph 5 are subject to the provisions of Article 41 of the Producer-Writers Guild Theatrical Basic Agreement of 1963 which provisions are herein incorporated by reference.

6. In addition to your services hereunder, we shall own, and you hereby transfer and assign to us, all rights of whatever kind and character throughout the world, in perpetuity, in any and all languages, in and to all of the results and proceeds of your services hereunder (including all rights throughout the world of production, manufacture, recordation and reproduction by any art, method or device, whether now known or hereafter devised), whether such results and proceeds consist of literary, dramatic, musical, motion picture, mechanical or any other form of works, themes, ideas, creations, products or compositions. Our rights to publish a book of your screenplay shall be subject to the same restrictions and shall not be greater than our rights in the novel
on which it is based.

Without in any manner limited or derogating from the generality of the foregoing, we shall have the right, but not the obligation, to use, adapt, change, revise, delete from, add to and/or rearrange the material or any part thereof written by you hereunder, and to combine the same with other works to any extent that we shall desire, and to change or substitute the title thereof together with the right to record and photograph the same with or without sound (including spoken words, dialogue and music synchronously recorded), and to reproduce, transmit, broadcast by radio and/or television, perform and communicate the same by any means now known or hereafter devised either publicly or otherwise.

You agree to execute and deliver to us upon exercise of our option for rights in said novel or thereafter whenever requested by us in connection with all material written by you hereunder a certificate in the following form:

"I hereby certify that I wrote, as an employee of , all literary material submitted by me in connection with a motion picture photoplay tentatively entitled . I further certify that all of said literary material was written by me in the regular course of my employment pursuant to an employment agreement dated the day of , 19 , and that said employer above named is the author thereof and is entitled to the copyright thereon (and all renewals thereof), with the right to make such changes therein and uses thereof as it may from time to time determine as such author."

You recognize that the provisions hereinafter set forth dealing with any other documents to be signed by you are not to be construed in derogation of our rights arising from the employer-employee relationship but are included because in certain jurisdictions and in special circumstances the rights in and to material which flow from the employer-employee relationship may not be sufficient in and of themselves to vest ownership in us.

Should we desire to secure further documents covering, quitclaiming or assigning all or any of the results and proceeds of your services hereunder, or all or any rights in and to the same, then you agree to execute and deliver to us any such documents at any time and from time to time upon our request therefor, and in such form as may be prescribed by us on our counsel; and without limiting the generality of the foregoing you agree to execute and deliver to us upon our request therefor an assignment of all rights in the form attached hereto marked Exhibit A and made a part hereof by reference, it being agreed that all of the representations, warranties and agreements made and to be made by you under said Exhibit A shall be deemed made by you as part of this agreement. Your failure to execute said certificate and/or documents shall not affect or limit any of our rights in and to the results and proceeds of your services hereunder.

7. On condition that you shall fully and completely keep and perform all of your obligations and agreements hereunder and the Photoplay shall be completed and distributed, we agree that credits for authorship by you shall be determined and accorded pursuant to the provisions of Schedule A of the Producer-Writers Guild Theatrical Basic Agreement of 1963 as it may be amended from time to time (hereinafter referred to as "the Basic Agreement") in accordance with its terms at the time of such determination. In the event we are not a party to the Basic Agreement at the time for the determination of such credits, then such determination shall be made and the credits shall be accorded in the same manner as provided for in said Schedule A, subject to our right to determine the contribution of each writer to the literary material for the Photoplay.

Subject to the foregoing provisions, we shall determine, in our discretion, the manner of presenting such credits. No casual or inadvertent failure to comply with the provisions of this paragraph, nor any failure of any other person, firm or corporation to comply with its agreements with us relating to such credits, shall constitute a breach by us of our obligations under this paragraph. Your rights and remedies in the event of a failure, omission or default constituting a breach by us under the terms of this paragraph, shall be limited to your rights, if any, to recover damages in an action at law, and in no event shall you be entitled by reason of any such breach to rescind this agreement or any of the rights granted to us hereunder, or to enjoin or restrain the distribution or exhibition of the Photoplay.

8. During the term of this agreement at such time or times and during such period or periods as it may be lawful for us to require you to do so, at our request and at your sole cost and expense, you shall remain or become and remain a member in good standing of the ten properly designated organization or organizations (as defined and determined under the applicable

law) representing persons performing services of the type and character to be performed by you hereunder. Nothing herein contained shall be construed to require the violation of any written agreement executed between us and the labor organization referred to herein which may be in effect at the time of the execution of this agreement and wherever there is any conflict between any provisions of this agreement and any such agreement, the latter shall prevail, but in such event the provision of this agreement affected shall be curtailed and limited only to the extent necessary to permit compliance with such agreement and if such agreement requires the payment of any additional compensation it shall be at the minimum rate permitted thereby. No monies due you under said labor organization agreement or under the within agreement are to apply and be a credit against any sums or rights elsewhere reserved in other agreements between you and us.

9. If by reason of accident, illness, mental or physical disability (hereinafter for convenience referred to as "illness"), you shall be incapacitated or prevented from fully performing your services hereunder or complying with each and all of your obligations and agreements hereunder, or if you shall fail, refuse or neglect to perform fully your services hereunder or to comply with each and all of your obligations and agreements hereunder, then your services shall be suspended during the period of such illness or failure, refusal or neglect; and no compensation shall accrue or be payable to you for or during the period of such suspension. Any refusal or statement by you, personally or through your agent, that you will refuse to keep or perform your obligations and agreements hereunder shall constitute a failure to keep and perform such obligation or agreement from the date of such refusal or indication of refusal. At our option, exercisable at any time prior to the expiration of the term hereof, we may extend such term for the period or periods of such suspension. Should we pay you any compensation for or during any period of suspension, as aforesaid, we shall not be deemed to have waived any of our rights hereunder, and we may apply such compensation against any compensation thereafter accruing or becoming due hereunder. We may terminate this agreement and all of our obligations hereunder if you shall fail, refuse or neglect to perform fully your services hereunder or to comply with each and all

of your obligations and agreements hereunder, or if you shall
be incapacitated or prevented by reason of illness, for a consecutive period of two (2) or more weeks, or for an aggregate
period of three (3) or more weeks, from fully performing your
services hereunder or complying with each and all of your
obligations and agreements hereunder; and if such termination
is based on your illness the compensation, if any, theretofore
accruing to you hereunder when paid shall be payment in full
of the compensation due you hereunder. We may exercise said
right of termination by reason of your illness (continuing for
the designated period) at any time during the occurrence of
such illness and during a period of three (3) days after the
ending of such illness. We may exercise said right of termination by reason of your failure, refusal or neglect at any time
during the occurrence of such failure, refusal or neglect and
during a period of seven (7) days after the date upon which
you shall report to us ready, willing, able and available to
render all of your services hereunder. Any period of suspension
provided for hereunder shall be deemed to have expired three
(3) days after the ending of any illness hereunder or seven (7)
days after you shall report to us ready, willing, able and available to render all your services hereunder after the occurrence
of a failure, refusal or neglect on your part. We may, at our
election, reduce the minimum period, if any, during which we
are obligated under the terms of this agreement to employ you
or pay you compensation by a period of time equal to the
aggregate of any periods of suspension hereunder, or any part
thereof. We may, at our election, by written notice to you,
terminate any suspension hereunder at any time prior to the
time herein specified except during the actual continuance of
your illness which incapacitates or prevents you from rendering
the services required or desired by us hereunder. During any
period of suspension provided for under this paragraph you
shall not render services of any kind to or for any person, firm
or corporation or for or on your own behalf. Notwithstanding
anything to the contrary herein contained, during any period
of suspension provided for hereunder, this agreement shall continue in full force and effect except as herein expressly specified
otherwise. You agree that we may recover by appropriate
action or may withhold from any compensation payable to you
hereunder the amount of actual damage caused us by your
failure, refusal or neglect to keep and perform all of your

obligations and agreements hereunder, but in no event shall such damage be more than the amount due hereunder plus $10,000.00. In the event we shall terminate this agreement by reason of your failure, refusal or neglect you agree to pay to us on demand an amount equal to all compensation theretofore paid to you hereunder.

If you should at any time during the term hereof, allege that you are, or if you should at any time actually be, incapacitated by illness or other disability from fully performing your services hereunder or complying with each and all of your obligations and agreements hereunder, then we shall have the right and privilege to have medical examinations of you made by such physician or physicians as we may designate.

10. If during the time when you are rendering or are obligated to render services for us hereunder we are hampered, interrupted or interfered with in any manner whatever in the preparation or production of the photoplay or in the conduct and operation of our business generally, by reason of any present or any future statute, law, ordinance, regulation, order, judgment or decree, whether legislative, executive or judicial (whether or not constitutional), act of God, earthquake, flood, fire, epidemic, accident, explosion, casualty, lockouts, boycott, strike, labor controversy (including but not limited to threat of lockout, boycott or strike), riot, civil disturbance, war or armed conflict (whether or not there has been an official declaration of war or official statement as to the existence of a state of war), act of a public enemy, embargo, delay of a common carrier, inability without fault on our part to obtain sufficient material, labor, transportation, power or other essential commodity required in the conduct of our business, or by reason of the death, illness, incapacity or disability of the director or any principal member of the cast of the photoplay, or by reason of any cause, thing or occurrence of a similar or dissimilar kind not within our control, (any of the foregoing being herein referred to as an "event of force majeure"), then we may, at our option, suspend your services for any period during which such event or events or force majeure shall continue and no compensation shall accrue or be payable to you for or during the period of such suspension. Should we pay you any compensation for or during any period

of suspension, as aforesaid, we shall not be deemed to have waived any of our rights hereunder and we may apply such compensation against any compensation thereafter accruing or becoming due hereunder. In the event any such suspension shall continue for a period or periods of eight (8) weeks in the aggregate, then either of us may elect to cancel and terminate this agreement by written notice of such election to the other. If you shall elect to cancel and terminate this agreement as aforesaid, such election shall not be effective in the event we shall resume the operation of this agreement within one week after actual receipt of such notice of election by the payment to you of compensation thereafter accruing or becoming due hereunder, or, if there shall be no such compensation accruing or becoming due hereunder, then by notifying you that the period of such suspension has expired as of the expiration of said one week period. In such event this agreement shall not be cancelled and terminated at your election but shall continue in full force and effect, on condition that you are then ready, willing, able and available to render your services hereunder, subject, however, to our right for other proper causes (including but not limited to the occurrence of a different event of force majeure) then or thereafter to withhold payment of your compensation or to suspend or terminate your employment hereunder in accordance with the suspension or termination provisions contained in this agreement. In the event of a termination of this agreement under the provisions hereof, each of us shall be released and discharged from and of any further obligations hereunder and the compensation, if any, theretofore accruing to you hereunder, when paid, shall be payment in full of the compensation due you hereunder. We may, at our election, by written notice to you, terminate any suspension hereunder prior to the time herein specified. During any period of suspension provided for under this paragraph, and provided you shall not then be in default under any of the terms and conditions of this agreement, you shall be free to render your services for any other person, firm or corporation or for or on your own behalf; provided, however, that we shall have the absolute right to recall you to render your services hereunder on seven days' notice, in which event you agree to report to us to render your services hereunder at the expiration of said notice. Notwithstanding anything to the contrary herein contained, this agreement shall continue in full force and effect during any period of suspension provided hereunder except as herein expressly specified otherwise. At our option, exercisable at any time prior to the expiration of the term hereof, we may extend such term for the period or periods of such suspension. Your right to compensation for your services under subparagraphs (f) and (g) of Paragraph 3 shall remain in full force and effect notwithstanding any suspension or termination. Further said suspension shall not affect your rights under any other contract with us. If, after we terminate this agreement under this Paragraph 10, we resume or recommence preparation or production of the photoplay, we shall give you written notice thereof and offer to resume the operation of this agreement provided you are available and notify us of such availability within three (3) weeks after our notice and offer to you.

11. We shall have the right to produce, cut, edit, add to, subtract from, arrange, rearrange and revise in any manner the photoplay and the material composed, submitted or interpolated by you hereunder, and you hereby waive any so-called "moral rights" of authors.

12. You acknowledge and agree that you have no right or authority to and you will not employ any person to serve in any capacity, nor contract for the purchase or rental of any article or material, nor make any commitment or agreement whereby we shall be required to pay any moneys or other consideration without our express written consent first had and obtained.

13. You give and grant to us the right and privilege to use your name, voice and/or likeness in connection with the Photoplay and the advertising, exploitation and/or exhibition of the same, in connection with commercial advertising and publicity tie-ups relating to the Photoplay, and in connection with any and all of the results and proceeds of your services hereunder. You agree that we shall have the sole and exclusive right to issue publicity concerning you with respect to your employment hereunder and the Photoplay.

14. We shall not be required to utilize your services hereunder or to utilize in any manner any of the results and proceeds of your services or to produce, release, or market the Photoplay, or to continue the release and/or distribution of the Photoplay in any country or territory if commenced. Nothing

contained herein shall be deemed to relieve us of our obligation to pay you the compensation payable to you pursuant to this agreement, subject to such rights of suspension, extension and termination as are provided for in this agreement.

15. The rights herein granted to us are irrevocable and without right of rescission by you or reversion to you under any circumstances whatsoever. The expiration or termination of this agreement on whatever grounds and by whomsoever effected shall not affect or impair the exclusive ownership by us of any material theretofore written by you hereunder or any other results, proceeds or benefits of services theretofore rendered by you hereunder, except that you have certain rights in said material in the event of our failure to exercise our option as set forth in the option agreement between you and us executed simultaneously herewith. In connection with the foregoing, it is expressly understood and agreed that in the event we terminate or cancel (or purport to terminate or cancel) this agreement or any other agreement entered into by and between you and us concurrently herewith, or as part of the same transaction (and even if such cancellation or termination, or purported cancellation or termination is ultimately determined by a court to have been without proper or legal cause or if it be ultimately determined by such court that we committed any material breach of any such agreement), then your rights and remedies, in any such event, shall be strictly limited to your right and remedy, otherwise available, to recover damages, and you shall not have the right to rescind this agreement or any such other agreement, or any of our rights hereunder or thereunder, with respect to any such material or results, proceeds or benefits of your services. Each and all of the several rights and remedies provided for in this agreement shall be construed as being cumulative and no one of them shall be deemed to be exclusive of the others or of any rights or remedies allowed by law. No waiver by us of any failure by you to keep any covenant or condition of this agreement shall be deemed to be a waiver of any preceding or succeeding breach of the same or any other covenant or condition or shall be deemed a continuing waiver.

16. If we shall require you to render your services on location, which shall be at any place more than fifty (50) miles from   or such other place as you may then permanently (as opposed to temporarily) reside, we agree

to furnish you transportation (whether it be one or more trips at our request during the term of your employment) to and from such place and meals and lodging accommodations while you are on location to render your services hereunder. Such transportation shall be first class if available, and in lieu of furnishing you meals and lodging accommodations, we shall pay you a living expense allowance at the rate of $35.00 per day.

17. From the inception of the term hereof and continuing throughout the production and distribution of the Photoplay you will conduct yourself with due regard to public convention and morals and will not do anything which will tend to degrade you in society or bring you into public disrepute, contempt, scorn, or ridicule or that will tend to shock, insult or offend the community or public morals or decency, or prejudice us or the motion picture industry in general. In the event of any breach of the terms hereof, we may, in addition to any other rights or remedies, terminate this agreement and/or refrain (insofar as permitted under any applicable guild agreements to which we are signatory producers) from giving you any credit in connection with the Photoplay if we are otherwise obligated to give you such credit.

18. You acknowledge that your services hereunder are of a special, unique, unusual, extraordinary and intellectual character, the loss of which cannot be reasonably or adequately compensated in damages in an action at law, and by reason thereof you agree that we shall be entitled to injunctive and other equitable relief to prevent or curtail any breach of this agreement by you.

19. Nothing contained in this agreement shall be construed so as to require the commission of any act contrary to law, and wherever there is any conflict between any provision of this agreement and any material statute, law, ordinance or regulation contrary to which the parties have no legal right to contract, then the latter shall prevail, but in such event the provision of this agreement so affected shall be curtailed and limited only to the extent necessary to bring them within the legal requirements. Each and all of the several rights and remedies provided for in this agreement shall be construed as being cumulative, and no one of them shall be deemed to be exclusive of the others or of any right or remedy allowed by

law. No waiver by either of us of any failure by the other to keep or perform any covenant or condition of this agreement shall be deemed to be a waiver of any preceding or succeeding breach of the same or any other covenant or condition.

20. You hereby consent and agree that we, as your employer, may deduct and withhold from your compensation the amounts to be deducted and withheld by us under the provisions of the Federal Income Tax and Social Security Acts, California Unemployment Insurance Act, any and all amendments thereto, and other statutes heretofore or hereafter enacted requiring the withholding of compensation. If the compensation provided by this agreement shall exceed the amount permitted by any present or future law or governmental order or regulation, then such compensation shall be reduced while such limitation is in effect to the amount which is so permitted; and the payment of such reduced compensation shall be deemed to constitute full performance by us of our obligations hereunder with respect to the payment of compensation for such period. You also authorize and instruct us to deduct from each installment of your compensation hereunder a sum equal to one percent (1%) of the gross amount thereof and to pay the said sum to the Motion Picture Relief Fund of America, Inc.

21. You expressly agree that we may transfer and assign this agreement or all or any part of our rights hereunder to any person, firm or corporation; and this agreement shall inure to the benefit of our successors, licensees and assigns. We agree to guarantee performance by any assignee or transferee of our obligations hereunder; provided, however, that we shall be relieved of any obligation hereunder if such obligations are assumed by an assignee or transferee who is one of the following companies or another company with not less than the financial responsibility of any of the following: Metro-Goldwyn-Mayer, Inc., Columbia Pictures Corporation, Warner Brothers Pictures, Inc., United Artists Corporation, Paramount Pictures Corporation, Twentieth Century-Fox Film Corporation, Universal Pictures, Buena Vista Film Distribution Co.

22. All notices which we are required or may desire to give to you hereunder may be served by delivering them to you personally or by sending them to you by mail or telegraph at , with copies to ,

or such other address as you may from time to time designate in writing. All payments to you hereunder shall be payable to

as agents for   ,

or to such other agent or place as you may from time to time designate in writing.

All notices which you are required or may desire to serve upon us hereunder may be served by delivering them to us by mail or telegraph at   , or at such other address as we may from time to time designate in writing.

Except as hereinafter expressly provided, the date of mailing or delivery to the telegraph office of such notice, as the case may be, shall be deemed the date of service of such notice. Notwithstanding the provision of the foregoing sentence, the literary and/or dramatic material required of you hereunder, and any notice or notices from you which commence the running of any period of time for the exercise by us of an option or the performance by us of any other act hereunder, shall be deemed to be delivered only when actually received by us.

23. This agreement (including any exhibits attached hereto) contains the full and complete understanding between us with reference to the within subject matter, supersedes all prior agreements and understandings whether written or oral pertaining thereto, and cannot be modified except by a written instrument signed by each of us. You acknowledge that no representation or promise not expressly contained in this agreement has been made by us or any of our agents, employees or representatives. This agreement in all respects shall be construed under and shall be subject to the laws of the State of California.

Your signature affixed at the place indicated will constitute this a binding agreement between us.

Very truly yours,

_____

ACCEPTED AND AGREED TO:

_____

Typical translation contract

MEMORANDUM OF AGREEMENT MADE THIS

day of   , 19   between

(hereinafter called the proprietor) of the one part

and

(hereinafter called the publisher) of the other part WHERE-
BY it is mutually agreed as follows regarding the work

by

entitled

1. The proprietor hereby grants to the publisher the sole
license to publish the said work in volume form in the

language in

subject to the following terms and conditions:

2. The publisher shall pay to the proprietor the sum of

on signature of this agreement, such sum to be in advance and
on account of a royalty on the published price of said work of

3. The publisher agrees to bring out his edition of said work
within eighteen (18) months of the date of this agreement.

4. Six gratis copies of the said translated work shall be sent
to the proprietor on publication.

5. The translation of the said work shall be made faithfully and accurately. Abbreviations or alterations in the text shall only be made with the written consent of the proprietor.

6. The title of said work in English shall appear beneath the title or on the back of the title page of every copy issued. Copyright notice shall be printed exactly as it appears in the American edition of the said work.

7. The publisher undertakes that the name of the author shall appear in its customary form in due prominence on the title-page and on the binding of every copy produced and on all advertisements of the said work issued by the publisher.

8. If the publisher fails to issue his edition of the said work within the term of eighteen months from the date of this agreement or if the translation of said work goes out of print or off the market, said agreement shall be automatically cancelled and the proprietor shall resume possession of the license granted to the publisher hereunder without prejudice to any monies already paid.

9. The term of this grant is for a period of six years from the date of this agreement at which time all rights herein granted shall automatically revert to the proprietor.

10. The license herein granted is assigned to the above named publisher solely and shall only be transferred by them with the written consent of the proprietor.

11. Should the publisher be declared bankrupt or should he violate any of the terms of this agreement, all rights to publish or sell the said work shall automatically revert to the proprietor.

12. In the event that the proprietor should license or sell the work for use in motion pictures, television and radio, the proprietor may grant motion picture, television and radio rights to the translation. Nothing in this agreement shall prevent the proprietor from publishing in any country in the said language extracts from or synopses of the said work not exceeding seventy-five hundred (7500) words in length for use in connection with the exploitation of motion pictures based upon the said work.

13. All rights not herein granted to the publisher either now existing, or which may hereafter come into existence are specifically reserved to the proprietor.

14. Accounts of sales of the said work shall be made up by the publisher each year to the 31st of December and shall be settled within ninety (90) days thereafter.

15. This contract shall not be valid until the advance on royalties due in respect to clause 2 of this agreement has been received.

16. All statements and monies due under this agreement shall be paid to the author's representative:

whose receipt shall be a discharge of the monies received and said representative is hereby empowered by the proprietor to conduct negotiations with the publisher in respect to all matters arising out of this agreement.

17.

. . . .
     Publisher   Proprietor

A sample form of release which television writers must sign when submitting scripts for possible purchase and use over the air.

RELEASE

XYZ Broadcasting System, Inc.   Date:
ooo Madison Avenue   Title of material
New York, New York   submitted:

Gentlemen:

I am today submitting to you program material upon the following express understanding and conditions:

1. I represent that the features which I have specifically described on page two hereof are original with me and that no persons other than those whose names appear below have collaborated with me in creating this material. I limit my claim of rights to such features and acknowledge that I do not, and will not, claim any rights whatsoever in any other elements of the program material which are not so described, unless such material embodies concrete literary expression in which case I claim rights in the manner of such expression. I claim exclusive rights in the title only as regards its use in connection with the elements of the program material submitted hereunder.

2. You will not use the material submitted by me hereunder unless (i) you shall first negotiate with me compensation for such use, or (ii) unless you shall determine that you have an independent legal right to use such material which is not derived from me, either because the material submitted hereunder is not new or novel, or was not originated by me, or has not been reduced to concrete form, or because other persons including your employees have submitted, or may hereafter submit, similar or identical suggestions, features and material which you have the right to use.

3. In the event that, pursuant to paragraph 2 above, you determine that you have the legal right to use any of the material

submitted by me hereunder without the payment of compensation to me and proceed to use the same, and if I disagree with your determination, I agree that, if you so elect, the dispute between us shall be submitted to arbitration, the arbitrator to be a person experienced in the radio or television fields, and mutually selected by you and me, or, if we cannot agree, then to be selected as provided by the rules of the American Arbitration Association. The Arbitration shall be controlled by the terms hereof, and any award favorable to me shall be limited to the fixing of a royalty which shall not exceed royalties normally paid by XYZ for a comparable program suggestion in the regular course of business.

Very truly yours,

(a) Name   (b) Name
          (PRINT)   (PRINT)
    Name   Name
          (SIGNATURE)   (SIGNATURE)
    Address   Address
    City   City
    Telephone No.:   Telephone No.:

NOTE: Sole owner should complete section (a). In a case of collaboration, one owner should complete section (a) and the other owner should complete section (b).

Executed on behalf of
as duly authorized agent.   (INSERT OWNER'S NAME)
Name of Agency
By
          (NAME OF AGENCY REPRESENTATIVE)
Address
City
Telephone No.:
Please indicate form of material submitted:

    Outline   ☐   Transcription ☐
    Script   ☐   Film   ☐
    Brochure   ☐   Other_____

SUMMARY OF MATERIAL SUBMITTED:

_____

_____

————————————————————————
————————————————————————
————————————————————————
————————————————————————
————————————————————————
————————————————————————
————————————————————————
————————————————————————
————————————————————————
————————————————————————
————————————————————————
————————————————————————
————————————————————————
————————————————————————
————————————————————————
————————————————————————
————————————————————————

(If space is insufficient, please complete summary on reverse side)

Received in accordance with the foregoing,
XYZ BROADCASTING SYSTEM, INC.
By_____

Organizations for Writers

Listed below are the principal trade organizations for professional writers. The two largest, the Authors League of America and the Writers Guild of America, have a large number of members who are not at the present time active writers making substantial money from their pens. The membership of all these groups fluctuates. All of them have associate members, such as editors, producers, agents, who are not writers and who have no voting powers. Some professional writers belong to more than one organization. Unfortunately, many active professional writers in the book and magazine field do not belong to any organization.

Each organization should be consulted as to specific eligibility requirements, various classes of membership, current dues, etc.

THE AUTHORS LEAGUE OF AMERICA, INC.
234 West 44th Street
New York, N.Y. 10036
This is the oldest and best known of all the writers' organizations. It is divided into two guilds:
THE AUTHORS GUILD
About twenty-eight hundred active writers. Dues $30 annually. Membership requirements: satisfactory evidence of publication in book or magazine field.
THE DRAMATISTS GUILD
About one hundred active dramatists. Dues $30 annually. Membership obligatory for an author under contract for a Broadway production.

THE WRITERS GUILD OF AMERICA, INC.
This has two affiliated branches:
WRITERS GUILD OF AMERICA, EAST, INC.
1212 Avenue of the Americas
New York, N.Y. 10036
About four hundred active writers, most of whom work in the TV field; a few work in radio or in motion pictures. Dues

$20 plus 1¼ per cent of earnings. Union shop. Membership obligatory after thirty days' employment.

WRITERS GUILD OF AMERICA, WEST, INC.
8955 Beverly Boulevard
Los Angeles, Calif. 90048
About two thousand active TV and motion picture writers plus a few in radio and in commercial films. Dues $20 plus 1¼ per cent of earnings. Union shop. Membership obligatory after thirty days' employment.

MYSTERY WRITERS OF AMERICA, INC.
151 West 48th Street
New York, N.Y. 10036
About five hundred active writers. Dues $20 annually. Has branches in Hollywood, San Francisco, and Chicago. Membership requirements: evidence of proficiency in the mystery field.

WESTERN WRITERS OF AMERICA, INC.
11 Kansas Avenue
Bend, Oregon 97701
About one hundred and twenty-five active members. Dues $15 annually. Membership requirements: extensive publication in the Western field.

THE SOCIETY OF MAGAZINE WRITERS
c/o Overseas Press Club
54 West 40th Street
New York, N.Y. 10018
About two hundred twenty-five active members. Dues $35 annually. Membership requirements: publication of articles in magazines of general circulation to demonstrate professional status.

Preparing and submitting a manuscript.

Writers should be familiar with certain mechanics connected with the preparation of a manuscript, and should always keep in mind that it is worthwhile to make a manuscript easy for an editor to read.

Offer editors manuscripts typed double-spaced on heavy white paper with wide margins and a minimum of handwritten corrections. Number the pages consecutively. There should be a title page containing the title, and the author's name and address. There is no need for the title or the author's name to be typed on each individual page.

Do not staple the pages together. No cover or folder for the manuscript is necessary—no one wants to use physical labor to keep a manuscript open. (An editor may read a few pages of a manuscript, and then be interrupted; he does not want the pages of the manuscript to close so that he has to hunt for his place.)

When mailing a manuscript, you may insert a piece of cardboard in the envelope if desired, to prevent the manuscript from getting creased. A large manuscript should be sent with the pages loose in a box. A brief manuscript should be held together with a paper clip; it may be mailed in a large envelope.

A short letter of transmittal should accompany a manuscript. This letter should never describe the piece. After all, the manuscript is to be read, and its fate will be determined after it has been read, and not by the author's advance description. Never give a sales talk about your wares. The editor presumably knows more about sales possibilities than the writer does.

A letter saying the following is often all that is necessary:

Dear Mr. ———:

    I am enclosing a story entitled ————— for your consideration. Return postage is enclosed.

Very truly yours,

Book manuscripts may be sent by Railway Express or by first-class mail. However, the most inexpensive and commonly used method is by the Special Fourth-Class Rate—Manuscript. At present, the postal regulations for this rate are as follows:

1. Manuscripts for books and periodicals may be mailed for 16¢ for the first two pounds or less and 6¢ for each additional pound or fraction, without regard to zone.

2. If the manuscript weighs less than two pounds, the two-pound rate of 16¢ may be applied, if the 16¢ rate is lower than postage at the first-class rate of 6¢ an ounce.

3. Envelopes and packages must be marked on the outside, *Special Fourth-Class Rate—Manuscript*. (Be sure stamped return envelopes are also marked *Special Fourth-Class Rate—Manuscript*.)

4. You may insure manuscripts marked *Special Fourth-Class Rate—Manuscript*, and secure a receipt at the post office. The rate for $50 worth of insurance is 30¢, and the fee for the receipt is 10¢, making a total fee of 40¢ in addition to the regular postage rate as above. Manuscripts may be insured up to $200; for rates, inquire at your post office.

5. Letters may not be enclosed with manuscripts at the above manuscript postage rates. If you wish to include a letter, you may do so, provided you state on the outside of the package that first-class material is enclosed, and place additional first-class postage (6¢ an ounce) on the package.

Return postage and a self-addressed envelope should be included with a short piece. The author may suggest that a long manuscript be returned by Express Collect.

Do not put on the manuscript or in your letter of transmittal anything about the rights for sale, or the rights reserved. The rights sold to a magazine are the rights the magazine regularly buys. With a book publisher, it is a matter for discussion after acceptance of the manuscript. Do not type a copyright notice on your manuscript. There is no way of copyrighting a book, short story, article or poem, except in connection with publication.

A manuscript after several declinations may get dog-eared. In such a case, retype it. An editor recognizes that a dirty, creased manuscript is one that has been read by many other editors, and declined several times. This reduces his interest. Why let the condition of the manuscript prejudice him?

It is important for an author to keep a carbon of every manuscript offered for sale. It is rare, but manuscripts do get lost; sometimes a few pages may disappear, or a manuscript may be mislaid and hence lost for several weeks. Remember that a publishing house will have several hundred manuscripts on hand at any one time. A magazine may have two thousand manuscripts being read. There have been classic losses of manuscripts before the advent of the typewriter and carbon paper. A servant of John Stuart Mill's destroyed the only copy of the first volume of Carlyle's *History of the French Revolution.* Five months work was wasted—and Carlyle had to write the manuscript a second time!

Society of Authors' Representatives code of ethics and membership list.

THE LITERARY AGENT

A literary agent is an author's business representative. As such, his main objectives are commercial, and it is his responsibility to protect his client's best interests. His relationship to a client is fiduciary. As an editorial advisor, he may offer an author literary criticism.

What The Agent Can Do For His Client

Negotiate sale or lease of certain rights in the work.

Reserve rights not essential to the negotiation in hand for later disposition in other markets. Many examples could be cited, but two typical ones would be the retention for author's benefit of motion picture rights in a book publication contract, or dramatic rights in a motion picture contract.

Examine contracts and negotiate modifications whenever justified.

Recommend contracts for author's approval and signature or recommend rejection, stating reason.

Collect monies due.

Examine royalty statements.

Check on publisher's handling of a book, including such details as manufacture, blurb copy, dust jacket, advertising and publicity.

Check on copyright.

Don't Expect Too Much. The Agent Cannot—

Sell unsalable work.

Teach a beginner how to write salable copy.

Act as editor of writer's work.

Solve author's personal problems or lend money.

Be available outside of office hours except by appointment.

Perform the functions of a press agent, social secretary or travel agent.

Although an agent may, on occasion, give informed legal and/or tax advice, he is neither licensed to practice law nor does he qualify as a tax expert.

Standard Practices of The Agent

1. He retains ten per cent commission on domestic sales and up to twenty per cent on foreign sales.

2. He pays out the author's share of monies promptly after receipt.

3. He charges the author with no expense incurred by the normal operation of his office. He does charge the author for such items as copyright fees, manuscript retyping, copies of books for submission overseas, long distance telephone calls and cables. Agent may reimburse himself for monies paid out for author from funds collected on author's account.

4. He maintains separate bank accounts so that monies due authors are not commingled with agency's working funds.

5. He does not advertise his services.

6. Some recognized agents may charge a nominal reading fee for unsolicited material, but will refund in event of sale of the material.

7. Most agents require authors to sign an agency agreement which spells out details of the author/agent relationship.

8. With power of attorney, he signs contracts in author's name when author is inaccessible.

9. He treats the financial affairs of his client as private and confidential.

Literary agents maintain working relationships with agents abroad, through whom the work of their clients is offered in appropriate markets. A literary agency is therefore essentially a service organization for the systematic marketing of literary properties.

Agency commission on business transacted in The British Commonwealth is usually fifteen per cent total, and on the European continent and elsewhere, twenty per cent.

Some agencies handle an author's work in all fields, including book and periodical publishing, theatre, motion pictures, radio and television. Other agents specialize in material for book and magazine publication only. The latter may work with other agencies to market subsidiary and extra rights. In such cases, the combined fees do not exceed ten per cent on domestic sales.

How To Find A Literary Agent

Agents prefer that authors write a short letter before sending in manuscripts, describing their work and giving a brief résumé of their interests. The author should make reference to any of his work which may have been published or performed.

Any of the following will supply a list of reputable agents:

1. The Authors Guild, 234 West 44 Street, New York, to its members.
2. Nationally known book publishers.
3. National magazines.

In 1928, a group of literary and play agents organized the Society of Authors' Representatives, Inc. This is a voluntary association of agents, each individual member of which subscribes to the ethical practices described herein.

The following is a list of the membership of the association.

Cyrilly Abels
597 Fifth Avenue
New York, N.Y. 10017
(L)

American Play Company, Inc.
52 Vanderbilt Avenue
New York, N.Y. 10017
(D)

Artists Agency Corporation
1271 Avenue of the Americas
New York, N.Y. 10020
(L-D)

Ashley Famous Agency, Inc.
1301 Avenue of the Americas
New York, N.Y. 10019
(L-D)

Bill Berger Associates, Inc.
535 East 72 Street
New York, N.Y. 10021
(L)

Lurton Blassingame
60 East 42 Street
New York, N.Y. 10017
(L)

Brandt & Brandt
101 Park Avenue
New York, N.Y. 10017
(L)

Curtis Brown, Ltd.
60 East 56 Street
New York, N.Y. 10022
(L-D)

James Brown Associates, Inc.
22 East 60 Street
New York, N.Y. 10022
(L-D)

Collins-Knowlton-Wing, Inc.
60 East 56 Street
New York, N.Y. 10022
(L)

Maurice Crain, Inc.
18 East 41 Street
New York, N.Y. 10017
(L)

John Cushman Associates, Inc.
24 East 38 Street
New York, N.Y. 10016
(L)

Joan Daves
145 East 49 Street
New York, N.Y. 10017
(L)

Ann Elmo Agency, Inc.
545 Fifth Avenue
New York, N.Y. 10017
(L-D)

Frieda Fishbein
353 West 57 Street
New York, N.Y. 10019
(L-D)

Harold Freedman
Brandt & Brandt Dramatic Depart-
    ment, Inc.
101 Park Avenue
New York, N.Y. 10017
(D)

Samuel French, Inc.
25 West 45 Street
New York, N.Y. 10036
(L-D)

Blanche C. Gregory, Inc.
2 Tudor City Place
New York, N.Y. 10017
(L)

Franz J. Horch Associates, Inc.
325 East 57 Street
New York, N.Y. 10022
(L)

Lucy Kroll Agency
119 West 57 Street
New York, N.Y. 10019
(L-D)

Robert Lantz Literary Agency
111 West 57 Street
New York, N.Y. 10019
(L-D)

Littauer & Wilkinson
500 Fifth Avenue
New York, N.Y. 10036
(L)

The Sterling Lord Agency
75 East 55 Street
New York, N.Y. 10022
(L-D)

Harold Matson Company, Inc.
22 East 40 Street
New York, N.Y. 10016
(L-D)

Monica McCall, Inc.
    Jo Stewart
667 Madison Avenue
New York, N.Y. 10021
(L-D)

McIntosh, McKee
    & Dodds, Inc.
22 East 40 Street
New York, N.Y. 10016
(L-D)

McIntosh & Otis, Inc.
18 East 41 Street
New York, N.Y. 10017
(L)

William Morris Agency, Inc.
1350 Avenue of the Americas
New York, N.Y. 10019
(L-D)

Harold Ober Associates,
 Incorporated
40 East 49 Street
New York, N.Y. 10017
 (L)

Gilbert Parker
600 Madison Avenue—19th Floor
New York, N.Y. 10022
 (D)

Paul R. Reynolds, Inc.
599 Fifth Avenue
New York, N.Y. 10017
 (L)

Virginia Rice
301 East 66 Street
New York, N.Y. 10021
 (L)

Flora Roberts, Inc.
22 East 60 Street
New York, N.Y. 10022
 (L-D)

Marie Rodell
141 East 55 Street
New York, N.Y. 10022
 (L)

Russell & Volkening, Inc.
551 Fifth Avenue
New York, N.Y. 10017
 (L)

Leah Salisbury, Inc.
790 Madison Avenue
New York, N.Y. 10021
 (L-D)

John Schaffner
896 Third Avenue
New York, N.Y. 10022
 (L)

Tams-Witmark Music Library, Inc.
757 Third Avenue
New York, N.Y. 10017
 (D)

Annie Laurie Williams, Inc.
18 East 41 Street
New York, N.Y. 10017
 (L-D)

Mary Yost Associates
141 East 55 Street
New York, N.Y. 10022
 (L)

(L: Literary Agent   D: Dramatic Agent)